Beatrice

The Untold Story of a Legendary Woman of Mystery

Sheldon Bart

NEWPORT LEGENDS, LLC

Newport Legends, LLC
2 Seaview Avenue
Newport, RI 02840

Library of Congress Catalog Card Number: 97-069778.
ISBN 0-9660285-0-3
Publisher's Cataloging-in-Publication Data:

Bart, Sheldon.
     Beatrice : the true story of Newport's legendary woman of
mystery / Sheldon Bart.—1st ed.
     p. cm.
     ISBN: 0-9660285-0-3

     1. Turner, Beatrice, 1888–1948. 2. Painters—Rhode
Island—Newport—Biography. 3. Women painters—Rhode
Island—Newport—Biography. 4. Painters—Pennsylvania—
Philadelphia—Biography. 5. Women painters—Pennsylvania—
Philadelphia—Biography.   I. title.

ND237.T87B37 1998   759.1974'57
                                     QB197-41036

Cover art by Beatrice Turner
Cover design by Barb Gunia
Book design and composition by Sans Serif, Saline, Michigan
Printed in the United States of America

THE LEGEND

This is the story of a beautiful woman and the mystery that surrounded her. A woman who was born to fabulous wealth and social position, whose life was a turmoil of suffering, loneliness, artistic triumphs and madness. Her strange death less than two years ago brought gasps of horror from America.

Can you imagine a woman who spent her entire lifetime looking in a mirror and creating thousands—yes, thousands—of paintings of herself?

Can you sympathize with a woman who was locked in her room for weeks, because, at the height of her romantic youth, she dared to be seen with a man?

Can you imagine a woman who for weeks refused to let her father's cold corpse be buried until she could paint his portrait in death?

Can you understand a woman who, for reasons known only to herself, one day ordered her house to be painted a gruesome black and lived with it that way for the rest of her life?

Can you picture a woman who right up until 1948 wore the clothes of the Victorian era until suddenly, just before her death, she cast them aside and painted herself in the nude?

This is not fiction. This really happened. This is fact. You have read about her in the greatest newspapers and magazines in America. Her eccentricities and her strange end puzzled a nation. No one could explain her. But after her death, in moldy diaries hidden away in ancient cupboards in her home, the answer was revealed.

Here is the story—the story of egosexia.

Her name was Beatrice Pastorius Turner. She was born in 1888 and died in 1948, after having lived as strange a life as has ever been lived.

—From a 1950 lecture by
Nathan Fleischer

Beatrice Turner self-portrait (1921) at age 33.

PROLOGUE

She was a solitary woman, beautiful, elegant and mysterious. Her hair was dark and she wore it up, piled under a broad, black picture hat such as might have adorned a Ziegfeld Follies star. She had an oval face that came to a delicate point at the chin. The soft blush on her cheeks had not been acquired from a cosmetics jar; she had a natural glow, a peaches-and-cream complexion. Her nose was straight. Her lips were full. Her eyes were large, dark and searching. There was an air of refinement, a sense of breeding in the way she held herself erect. She was sleek, slender and shapely, and looked smashing in the high-waisted dresses and ankle-length skirts that were in vogue when she came of age. She retained her stunning looks and willowy figure through middle age. Her manners remained scrupulously correct, her personal life untainted by scandal. But, for some largely impenetrable reason, she continued to wear clothes that had been fashionable in the gracious era prior to World War I. She dressed this way even after the manic decade of the Roaring Twenties had been succeeded by the Great Depression and the Second

World War. She never had a lover; according to some reports, she scarcely had a friend. The social arbiters of Philadelphia, Pennsylvania, her winter residence, and Newport, Rhode Island, her summer home, were openly contemptuous. They seriously doubted her sanity. Certainly there were ample grounds for those suspicions.

Just after her death almost fifty years ago, Beatrice Turner was the subject of a shocking exhibition held at one of the great Newport mansions. Many of the people who attended the show knew her from a distance. There are still today, almost fifty years later, people who remember her. Due to an altogether improbable chain of events going back over five decades now, a growing number of people have heard of her and are familiar with her work. No one, it seems, actually *knew* her, knew her intimately, knew what made her tick. No one.

Recollections come easily to those who knew her, say, by sight or in passing. She left indelible impressions:

A wistful, strikingly attractive society woman accompanied to the theatre only by her stone-visaged mother, both attired in late Victorian eveningwear decades out of date.

A solitary figure on an oceanfront walk, a Charles Dana Gibson figure in a flapper age, gazing out upon the thrashing waves.

A lonely, reclusive beauty standing before an easel erected on her veranda, a paintbrush in one hand, a small mirror in the other, working, with the assurance of a professional, on a life-size self-portrait.

A handsome, ageless, genteel chatelaine, dressed in white as if for a Victorian high tea, mowing the manicured lawn of her summer estate, having carefully wrapped pieces of paper around the wooden handles of the lawnmower to prevent them from soiling her white gloves.

A rambling mansion whose entire exterior had been—and remained for the last thirty-five of her forty-one years of occupancy—painted black.

People talked, as people will, and wherever she went, Beatrice Turner heard the whispers, but never raised her voice. She was, in truth, a highly intelligent, gifted, sensitive soul, a single woman and an artist who lived and worked in a restrictive age. The nature of the body of work to which she dedicated herself was largely unsuspected, so that the truth, ultimately, was stranger than the gossipmongers might have supposed. For this reason, although she died in obscurity, she has, almost since the moment of her death, continued to fascinate those acquainted with the facts of her life.

Beatrice Turner self–portrait (1908) at age 20.

I

*E*ight years ago, Winthrop P. Baker, a former president of General Electric Broadcasting and Cable, a former president of the TV Group of Westinghouse Broadcasting, and an influential production executive who had helped pioneer the long-form talk show and "reality TV," who had worked with Mike Wallace and Steve Allen, and had given Tom Snyder, Bill O'Reilly and Oprah Winfrey their first talk-show assignments, stood looking at a life-size painting in the parlor of a Victorian manor house in Newport, Rhode Island.

Baker had retired from broadcasting partly as a result of the Watergate-era investigations of corporate misconduct. RKO General Inc., a subsidiary of the General Tire and Rubber Company, had been ordered by the FCC to divest itself of WNAC-TV, a television station it owned and operated in Boston, Massachusetts, and had appealed the ruling to the U.S. Supreme Court. The FCC had charged that RKO General had failed to disclose that the parent company was under investigation for illegal political contributions. This was only the second time in the history of the FCC that it revoked a

Double self-portrait: Beatrice Turner and her mother Adele Tull Haas Turner, photographed in the parlor of Cliffside Inn in 1989. This is the only Turner painting that has never been removed from the house.

commercial license in a major market. The Court turned the appeal down without comment in 1982.

Baker was then president of New England Television, a local group that acquired the station and operated it as WNEV(TV). This group was subsequently replaced by another in a leveraged buy-out. The eventual settlement made Baker financially secure for the rest of his life. He formed an independent production company that created reality television programs dealing with subjects that included minority concerns and the plight of AIDS patients, and had gotten into the inn business on a lark when he and a colleague bought a property on the west coast while producing a TV show in San Francisco.

He was in Newport in 1989 looking for a property within a three-hour drive of his home in Wilton, Connecticut. A couple of bed-and-breakfast establishments were up for sale in Newport on that occasion. One was the Cliffside Inn, a flavorful hideaway near the famous Cliff Walk and a ten-minute stroll from the fabled Bellevue Avenue mansions. The painting that caught his eye came with the house.

It was a huge dual portrait completed in 1921 and depicting the occupants of the house at that time: a beautiful, wistful-looking woman in her early thirties, Beatrice Turner, and her mother, Adele Tull Haas Turner, both women attired in late Victorian eveningwear. The figures were so drawn that at first glance Mrs. Turner appears to be leading Beatrice by the hand. This is not so, but one has to look twice to be sure. Mrs. Turner, shown in profile, is looking off into the wings. Beatrice is glancing forward, responding to something of which only she is aware. It is a haunting, exquisite composition, and it was signed by Beatrice Turner.

The Turner estate, Cliffside, had been operated as a bed-and-breakfast inn since the 1970s. Kathleen Russell, the woman who owned the property at the time of Baker's visit, showed him an article clipped from the July 10, 1950 issue of *LIFE* magazine: "Lonely Spinster Paints 1,000 Portraits of Herself." It was illustrated with numerous self-portraits of Beatrice Turner and also included a photograph of a young man named Nathan Fleischer who was said to be exhibiting the paintings around the country. Mrs. Russell then handed Baker an audiocassette to listen to at his leisure. The cassette was affixed with a homemade label that read: "Nathan Fleischer - 1950."

Baker nodded. He had other things on his mind. He got back in his car,

This signature double portrait has been displayed at Cliffside since it was painted in 1921.

slipped the cassette into the tape deck and pulled out of the driveway. "This is the story of a beautiful woman and the mystery that surrounded her," the tape began. The narrator spoke with the arch intonation of a radio announcer of the *Inner Sanctum* era. "This is not fiction. This really happened. This is fact," he said. "Here is the story—the story of *e-go-sex-i-a*."

Win Baker had a beautiful wife, three grown sons and a lovely, woodsy home off a cozy byway in Connecticut. A trim, relaxed, literate man with a polished, Bill Moyers look, a whimsical smile and the buttoned-down manner of a popular college professor, he had gotten out of broadcasting because he understood that cable and pay-per-view services had changed the rules of the game and that the people he was dealing with were headed for trouble because they were clinging to outmoded assumptions about the future of broadcasting. At this stage of his life he was looking for a sensible way to invest some money and spend his time, and anticipated nothing more eventful than the challenge of redeveloping a historic Newport home into a luxurious inn.

He pulled off the road and listened to the story that unfolded on the tape, and found it so absorbing, so interesting and so provocative that for the moment he lost track of the world outside of his car. He didn't want to do anything else but sit there and hear the story through, and what he heard ultimately changed the course of his life.

Beaturice Turner self–portrait (1910) at age 22.

II

eatrice Pastorius Turner was born on December 10, 1888, and was the only child of a well-to-do Philadelphia couple. Her father had position, and her mother had a pedigree. Andrew J. Turner was a successful cotton broker. Adele Tull Haas Turner could trace her ancestry back to the sixteenth century. She was eighth in line of descent from Francis Daniel Pastorius, founder of Germantown, Pennsylvania, and sixth in line from Jacob Shallus, a Revolutionary War patriot who inscribed the Constitution of the United States.

The Turners were "main line," but they weren't millionaires, nor were they listed in the *Social Register*. They lived in a neighborhood, however, where many of the residents could claim both distinctions. They owned a handsome, four-story townhouse at 2322 Spruce Street, on the sunny southeast corner of 24th Street in central Philadelphia, one block from Schuylkill River Park. Among their neighbors were the city's most prominent bankers, attorneys, public officials, business executives, publishers and celebrities. Henrietta Meade, last surviving child of Major General George G. Meade, commander of the Union forces at the battle of Gettysburg, lived right across the street.

Adele Tull Haas Turner and Andrew Turner
double portrait by Beatrice Turner (c.1911).

Beatrice was educated at private schools and by governesses. At 16, she entered the Pennsylvania Academy of the Fine Arts in Philadelphia and showed promise. One of her teachers was the eminent Thomas Anshutz, a disciple of nineteenth-century America's leading realist painter, Thomas Eakins. Eakins had created a stir in art education by borrowing from the curriculum of medical school: he taught anatomy by dissecting cadavers. Anshutz modified the Eakins technique. He would mold a piece of clay into the shape of a muscle and mount the clay in the appropriate place on a human skeleton. Then he would point out the same muscle on a semi-nude live model standing by. Bearice Turner had aspirations of going to Europe and becoming a portrait painter. But at 18 she was forced to discontinue her studies because her parents would not allow her to behold Thomas Anshutz's models. About this time—1907—the Turners bought picturesque Swann Villa, a twin-towered, three-story Newport manor house, as a summer retreat.

The Villa—modest by Bellevue Avenue standards, the boulevard of Vanderbilts and Astors—was built in 1876 and occupied in 1877 by Congressman Thomas Swann of Maryland, a former governor of Maryland. It later served as the first campus of St. George's School, one of New England's most prestigious prep schools. St. George's leased the house and grounds from 1897 to 1901, when it moved to its present location in Middletown, Rhode Island. Modern owners have trimmed the building somewhat, lopping off a tower, a ballroom and other architectural flourishes, but even in its edited form the composition retains an engaging sweep. The Pulitzer Prize-winning poet Leonard Bacon, who attended St. George's in its Swann Villa days, said the Villa, as he remembered it, "was of a sort to make an indelible if equivocal impression on any mind, for it belonged to an obviously vanishing Newport, which in turn belonged in a novel by Edith Wharton. At first glance it seemed to consist entirely of attics and verandas." In those days, the grounds ran clear down to the Cliffs, overlooking the Atlantic Ocean. The Turners renamed the estate "Cliffside." Andrew Turner, apparently something of a neoclassicist, privately called it "Arcadia."

There was trouble in Arcadia. Andrew's relationship with his daughter was curious and disturbing. He did not allow Beatrice to have boyfriends, reportedly punished her for taking a stroll along Newport's famous Cliff Walk with a beau, and entertained some rather unfatherly thoughts, which he expressed in verse:

When looking at thy form divine
Perfect in each curve and line
And gazing at thy silken hair
And basking in thy orbits rare
A misnomer 'twas in naming thee
Aught else but Venus

Andrew Turner died in Philadelphia at the end of the summer season of 1913. He had returned to Philadelphia on a Saturday late in September to open the Spruce Street townhouse; his wife and daughter remained in Newport. He was found dead the next day. Before he died, he had written a poem:

I dreamed that I dwelt in a house of black
Located in the land of Arcadia
And absolutely nothing did it lack
For I was with my two sweethearts

I awoke and found I was in a house of brown
Far from loving glances and melodious voices
O when we are so far from those that we love
Don't such dreams last until we meet again?

The "house of brown" was obviously the brownstone townhouse at 2322 Spruce Street. But the "house of black" must have seemed inexplicable to the Turner women. Newport, carefree and bucolic in the years prior to World War I, was the "land of Arcadia" where Andrew had left his "two sweethearts," but Cliffside was patently not a "house of black." Why did he picture it that way? Did he know he was going to die? Spiritualism was very much in vogue in polite society in this period. Could mother and daughter have been persuaded that these lines were written *after* he died? In any event, for reasons that have not been clarified to this day, the Turners apparently interpreted the poem to mean that Cliffside must *become* a "house of black" and had it painted black. Their Newport neighbors were aghast. Naturally, they were unaware of the poem. Matters weren't helped by the fact that Beatrice had painted a portrait of her father in death. She was then 25. There were rumors that she had had

Cliffside (c. 1880) The house was then known as "Swann Villa".
It was built in 1876 as a summer home by Maryland Governor Thomas Swann.

The hand-written copy of Andrew Turner's birthday poem to Beatrice (1912).

Portrait of Adele Tull Haas Turner by her daughter Beatrice.

the embalmed remains propped in a chair and supported by pillows to accomplish this, and that she would not permit the burial to take place until the portrait was finished. The house was not repainted in Beatrice Turner's lifetime.

Beatrice's mother, Adele, was another gothic character. The dowager affected fragility and an inability to manage her own affairs. When her father passed away, Beatrice did what she had been trained to do since the cradle: she looked after her mother's needs and neglected her own. She became a financial consultant, housemaid, gardener and companion to her mother. The Turners attended social functions together. They were not on the "A" list. Or the "B." The smart set stood aloof and snickered, calling the Turners the "Century Ladies," because of their turn-of-the-century wardrobes. Beatrice never bobbed her hair or raised her hemline. Of course, if the Turners had lived in a palace and had millions to lavish on entertainments, their eccentricities might have been more graciously indulged.

After her mother's death in 1940, Beatrice continued to spend winters in

Cliffside in 1948, after Beatrice's death. The building was a run-down shamble still painted black.

Some of the 3,000 Beatrice Turner paintings that filled every space in the house when executors of the estate unlocked the doors.

Philadelphia and summers in Newport. In 1941 she exhibited a still life, "In a Drawingroom," at the annual summer exhibition of the Art Association of Newport and won the People's Prize, an award bestowed on the most popular painting. In succeeding years, she exhibited portraits of the Reverend Dr. Stanley Carnaghan Hughes, rector of Trinity Church and Jeannette R. Piccard, wife and co-pilot of the Swiss balloonist Jean Piccard and a member of a prominent Newport family. In 1943 Beatrice Turner became a member of the Plastic Club, a women's art club in Philadelphia, and exhibited the Piccard portrait and other works at this group's annual winter and spring exhibitions. She was one of three women elected vice presidents of the Plastic Club in 1946. Despite such mild forays into acceptance, Beatrice reportedly lived a reclusive and frugal existence. She died of cancer at University Hospital in Philadelphia on August 3, 1948.

In a scene only David O. Selznick could have dreamed of, when the executors of the estate mounted the black steps to the black porch, inserted the key in the lock and flung open the black double doors of Cliffside, they found ringing the walls of every room of the three-story mansion, piled from floor to ceiling in every room and stacked on every shelf of every closet, some three thousand oil paintings, watercolors and pencil sketches signed by Beatrice Turner. Beatrice had painted steadily all of her life. She painted exquisitely, and most of the time she painted herself! The vast majority were self-portraits. She painted herself sitting, she painted herself standing, she painted herself at home, she painted herself on the town, she painted herself in evening gowns, she painted herself in dressing gowns—and after her mother died she painted and sketched herself in the nude.

That wasn't all. In the cupboards and strewn on the floor were numberless black-bound volumes of a diary Beatrice had apparently kept for every day of every year of her adult life.

Amazingly, a swashbuckling character arrived in time to save some of this material from oblivion.

Beatrice Turner self–portrait (1914) at age 26.

III

*I*f the circumstances of his life had been slightly different, if he had had the necessary connections, if perhaps on any given street corner he had only turned left instead of turning right, Nathan Fleischer might have been famous. He might have been a celebrated showman or a successful politician. Certainly he had the prerequisites: intelligence, wit, charm, vision, energy, personality. He was a handsome devil who never stood pat and never stood still, although severe diabetes often forced him to slow down. A Jewish lawyer from New York City, he arrived in Newport in 1941 to open a branch of the family business, Worth Furs. He was 30 years old.

While in Newport, he represented a Syracuse businessman who had acquired Cliff Lawn, the estate down the block from Cliffside. The showpiece mansion had been erected in the Gilded Age by social luminaries John Winthrop Chanler and his wife, the former Margaret Astor Ward. But it had become something of a white elephant. The Syracuse man and the City of Newport were squabbling over taxes. When the dispute was settled, Fleischer was asked if he would accept Cliff Lawn in lieu of a check. Fleischer said, "Holy cow!"

He was small, sharp, wiry and engaging, and full of ideas and enthusiasms. In 1946 he devised a forward-looking, "environmentally aware" blueprint for a waterfront esplanade and other civic improvements to assure that Newport, a Navy town, would prosper in the postwar economy. In 1948 and again in 1950, he ran for mayor of Newport as

Attorney Nathan Fleischer (1949).

an independent and reformer—a Ross Perot-style candidate who promised to "get things done." He went on the radio in 1948 and invited his listeners to sit as a jury in what he called "the trial of the people of the City of Newport against the politicians." He then indicted the politicians on several charges including "extravagant waste of taxpayer money," "carelessly keeping and negligently permitting city property to rot," and "stifling the growth of city industry."

He was particularly forceful on graft. "Thirty-two times," he said in this address, he had asked the Republican and Democratic candidates, "'What deal did you make with the gambling interests of Newport so that they can continue to exist day by day?' Thirty-two times I got the same answer—absolute and complete silence." He started another radio address by announcing that he wasn't speaking from a prepared text. "I want you to feel as if I came into your living room to have a little chat with you," he told his audience. "Now, if I came into your house, I wouldn't bring a written speech with me!"

Fleischer's campaigns were rollicking affairs. One of his torchlight motorcades featured a Saint Bernard riding in the back seat of a convertible driven by the reigning Miss Newport; signs on the fenders hammered home the contention that Newport was "going to the dogs." The emblem of Fleischer's reform party, the Better Government Party, was a minuteman, and he had someone dressed in Revolutionary War getup at the head of another motorcade, on horseback. The minuteman was followed by a horse and buggy carrying a sign that said, "Do You Want This Type of Government?" Immediately behind the carriage came a streamlined automobile with the sign: "Or This?" Fleischer al-

Nathan Fleischer compaigning for mayor of Newport before a group of potential supporters: "I'd rather be mayor of Rogers High School than mayor of Newport."

ways finished a credible third. His best showing was in a mock election at Rogers High School in Newport which he won by a landslide. "I would rather be mayor of Rogers High School than mayor of Newport," he said.

Nathan Fleischer and Beatrice Turner lived within two hundred yards of each other during the last several summers of Beatrice's life, had an unobstructed view of each other's grounds and a nodding acquaintanceship. When the executors of the Turner estate were unable to dispose of Beatrice's accumulated paintings and drawings through bequests, or at a public auction—nobody wanted them—they arranged to have the three thousand compositions taken to the city dump and burned. Nathan Fleischer suddenly appeared and rescued at least sixty (conceivably as many as one hundred) works of art from certain destruction.

Two longtime Newporters who were close to Fleischer offer conflicting (but not mutually exclusive) interpretations of his gallantry. One, a southern gentleman, said, "Nathan had an eye for the females. And Miss Turner . . . she was a gooood-lookin' woman." The other said, "He thought he could make a dollar." In any event, between mayoral campaigns, Fleischer exhibited the collection at Cliff Lawn, which he had turned into a hotel, the Cliff Lawn Manor (now known as the Cliff Walk Manor). He charged an admission fee—three dollars, according to one of his old friends—and played up the elements of mystery and revelation.

Fleischer drew upon material in Beatrice's diaries to round out a 25-minute presentation on her life and work. He delivered the lecture himself, but not "in person." Huge, dark draperies were hung to screen off and backdrop the paintings. At each showing, Fleischer would conceal himself behind the folds of the draperies, creating the illusion of a disembodied voice. His lecture survives today. He had gotten tired of standing behind the draperies and orating, and decided to make a phonograph record that could be played for each group of paying customers that came to see the paintings. He made the record at the Newport home of the brilliant New England photographer John T. Hopf, a close friend. Fleischer had first tried to get Hollywood star Basil Rathbone to make the record. Rathbone had played Sherlock Holmes in an enormously popular series of movies. He was appearing at the Casino Theatre in Newport at the time, but he wanted $1,000 for his trouble, and Fleischer didn't have $1,000.

John Hopf later re-recorded the Fleischer lecture on audiocassette. This was the cassette that Win Baker slipped into his dashboard tape deck—curious but unsuspecting—when he pulled out of the driveway after his first visit to the Cliffside Inn. The original session had been recorded in Hopf's living room, but it didn't sound homemade. It was an impressive effort. Fleischer and Hopf's frame of reference was radio. They sought to replicate the production values of a radio show and were endlessly resourceful. Their choice of background music was inspired: Richard Strauss' moody, eerie, haunting, romantic "On the Beach at Sorrento." Nathan's voice had presented a problem; he felt it was too thin and reedy. That's why he wanted to hire Basil Rathbone. Hopf compensated by carrying in a large metal garbage can from outside. Fleischer stuck his head and the microphone inside the garbage can to record his narration, using the echo of the metal to add resonance to his voice. The piece opens with the strains of "Sorrento," then Nathan is heard, speaking over the music. *"This is the story of a beautiful woman and the mystery that surrounded her . . ."*

Cliff Lawn in 1950. The building is now a hotel, Cliff Walk Manor.

Nathan Fleischer at his Cliff Lawn art show with Turner paintings in background.

Nathan Fleischer using a garbage can to add resonance to his voice during the recording session at John Hopf's house.

Nathan's take on Beatrice was more than a shade on the lurid side. He invented a psychological concept to explain Beatrice's obsession with her own image—"egosexia"—and repeated this diagnosis several times in his narrative. He seems to mean by this something of an advanced case of narcissism. "There were times when she tried to be a happy girl," he said, discussing Beatrice's upbringing. "You've been told of her imprisonment when she tried to walk on Newport's famous Cliff Walk with a man. Can you imagine the effect upon a romantic, sensitive beauty to be punished for behaving normally? She was not allowed to love anyone. There was no one to love but herself. That's what psychologists call a Narcissus complex. That's egosexia."

Beatrice Turner appeared in this production by proxy. A young woman playing the part of Beatrice read excerpts from the diaries. No one today has any idea who she was, but she read her lines with an appropriately airy, lady-like, drawing-room trill, and her interpretations of such passages as the following were effective:

Ma-ma says I'm a nasty little dog and that not being strong enough to fight the world I fight her. A charming speech, which rather proves that the modern method of fending for oneself and refusing to be tied down by one's elders has it strong points.

Here I have been denied study at the art schools and a life of my own, have more or less cheerfully done housework since the age of eighteen that Ma-ma might continue her life in its groove—

Because I was not capable of doing anything else?

After deliberately taking me from my work, chaining me to her side all these years, years of being a coachman for her, years of housework, years of collecting life insurance, tending to investments—all of which she "could not do without me"—days and days, years and years of unselfish, rarely protesting obedience and patient endurance of whims—

Now having used up the fourteen best years of my life according to her whims—now it's because I am "too weak to have done otherwise"!

Howlingly funny. Slightly tragic for me.

When Fleischer gave this talk at the Cliff Lawn Manor, he apparently arranged for different Turner portraits to be highlighted or unveiled as he went along. The recorded lecture includes references to certain Turner art works—for example, a double portrait of Beatrice and her mother that sounds exactly like the painting Win Baker saw when he walked into the Cliffside Inn. "See the painting of the two of them together," Fleischer says. "See the

Nathan Fleischer's take on Beatrice was more than a shade on the lurid side.

dominating mannerisms of her mother leading her daughter by the hand. Those who knew Beatrice say that she seldom went anywhere without dear mama." He introduced Beatrice's nude studies, painted in the late 1940s, after the death of her domineering mother, this way: "As if stripping herself of the bonds of Victorianism, she stripped her clothes! This is the result. This is the honest portrayal of a woman of 59 years. Until these closing moments of her life, she would not cross the line. But egosexia overcame her. She loved her body, and she painted it for all to see."

He combined all of these themes—freedom, nudity, eroticism—in a fantastic conclusion describing the destruction of the three thousand paintings. "Heaped on a mound, they were ignited. They were the symbols of egosexia. They were the nude portraits, the final attempts of Beatrice to be free. And the flames of passion licked them away, licked the flesh from the canvas, searing what remained of a beautiful woman. This was the ghastly finish to egosexia, to Beatrice Turner, and from the flames that roared that night in Newport, you have seen here the afterglow. All that remains is around you, these few pages from her diary, these few paintings virtually snatched from the flames."

He knew how to sell a story, and the print media bought it. At least two national publications covered the Turner retrospective. *The American Weekly*, the graphic Sunday supplement of the *New York Journal-American*, *Boston Advertiser*, *Baltimore American* and other links in the Hearst newspaper chain, broke the story on November 6, 1949, and predictably reduced it to tabloid fodder. ("At Last Death Answers the Question Which Puzzled Newport: Why Did the Beautiful Heiress Spend 40 Years Locked Up in Her Lonely Jet-Black House?") *LIFE* magazine ("Lonely spinster paints 1,000 portraits of herself") told the story in pictures, with an eye-catching photospread of selected self-portraits.

Nathan Fleischer had taken the show on the road by the time the *LIFE* spread appeared (July 10, 1950). He loaded the paintings in a trailer and drove south to Miami Beach, but the traveling exhibit did not excite as much interest as he had hoped. He returned to Newport, ran for mayor for the second (and last) time, lost and shortly departed for greener pastures.

Fleischer later became a professional hypnotist and performed at Grossinger's, the Catskill Mountains resort, as "The Amazing Nathan Fleischer." In 1966, at the age of 55, he received a doctorate in psychology from

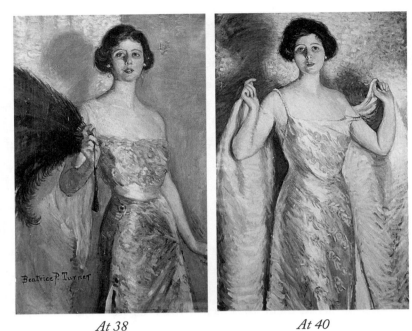

At 38   *At 40*

*These six photographs were featured in a July 10, 1950 LIFE
magazine article about Beatrice Turner. The five Turner paintings
were arrayed in the same chronological age sequence shown here
in order to depict how Turner portrayed her own aging process
over a 20 year period (1926–1946).*

Yeshiva University in New York. A couple of years later, he opened an office at
11 Fifth Avenue in Greenwich Village, and gained renown in the 1970s and
1980s as a hypnotherapist specializing in addiction and weight control. He
was the subject of a cover story in the July, 1977 issue of *Cosmopolitan*: "The
Amazing Diet of Dr. Fleischer—Removes Pounds but Not Curves!" The
amazing Nathan died in San Diego, California in 1990. As A. J. Liebling, the
great *New Yorker* writer and chronicler of Colonel John R. Stingo and other
picaresque characters, would say, "He lived a long and variegated life."
Liebling would have loved Nathan Fleischer. He leaves our story here.

At 44

At 46

At 58

Nathan Fleischer at one of his 1950 Beatrice Turner exhibits,
with his salvaged collection of Turner paintings.

Beatrice Turner self-portrait (1918) at age 30.

IV

One soggy spring day in the late 1980s, two Newport men, A.J. Sardella, Jr. and Anton Vasak, happened to be driving in A. J.'s VW down Broadway, which slants through Newport, and were approaching the intersection of Broadway and Rhode Island Avenue. They saw a huge pile of art works lying on the sidewalk at the corner of Rhode Island Avenue. This was an annual citywide "spring cleaning" day; people all over town had cleaned out their closets, attics and garages, and put the assorted clutter on the street for pick-up. A dump truck was slowly making its way along the same route that A. J. and Tony had taken, and was just a few minutes behind them. A. J. and Tony were inveterate collectors. They pulled over to the curb, got out of the car and poked through the pile.

It had been raining. The watercolors in the collection were ruined, a stack of charcoal sketches were sopping wet, but the oil paintings, some nearly lifesize canvasses, were unharmed. They were all signed by the same artist—Beatrice Turner—and almost all were portraits of the same subject: a beautiful

Tony Vasak and A.J. Sardella.

woman of a bygone, elegant era. The compositions seemed to resonate with a certain charm and vitality . . .

Tony stood guard over the paintings while A. J. went home to get his truck. When A. J. got back, he and Tony loaded the truck with as many paintings as it could hold—about sixteen—and took them back to A. J.'s house, which is just large enough to comfortably accommodate the various antiques, knickknacks, tchotchkes, and odds and ends they delight in accumulating. One painting blew off the truck on their way home.

When Nathan Fleischer left Newport, he did not take the sixty-plus paintings and drawings he had rescued with him. He left them at the home of a friend, Newport businessman Sidney Rosenthal. Rosenthal lived on Rhode Island Avenue, and had been Nathan's campaign manager in the two mayoral races. For years, the only substantial collection of Beatrice Turner's art currently known to have survived the bonfire had gathered dust in Rosenthal's attic and basement. When Rosenthal died and the Rhode Island Avenue house was sold, the Rosenthal family reluctantly put the collection out on the street for pick-up because they had nowhere else to put it.

A. J. and Tony had never heard of Beatrice Turner or Nathan Fleischer, and they didn't know that the paintings they had salvaged had narrowly escaped destruction for yet a second time. Nor did they know that the woman whose image now surrounded them, the beautiful woman in the large hat and gorgeous gowns, *was* Beatrice Turner, or anything about her. They might never have known.

Beatrice Turner self–portrait (1920) at age 32.

V

Win Baker bought the Cliffside Inn on September 1, 1989, and became the fifth person to own Cliffside since the death of Beatrice Turner. Mrs. Elizabeth C. Meikle, a warm, stout and universally beloved Newport woman, acquired the property early in 1949 from the Turner estate. The sprawling "house of black" was then in a state of disrepair. Mrs. Meikle restored Cliffside, but with a rather free hand. When she was finished, the ballroom was gone, and the veranda that had originally encircled the house was now a sedate front porch. Mrs. Meikle repainted the exterior and operated the property as a nursing home. She died in 1969.

A year later, Russell L. Cozzens, her son by a previous marriage, applied for a variance to turn Cliffside into a guest house. In Newport at that time, you had to apply for a variance if you wanted to rent rooms to more than four people. The property had apparently been in transition from nursing home to guest house before Mrs. Meikle died and Cozzens applied for his variance. Presumably less than four rooms had been let during this period. One of the occupants was Mary Healy, a teacher who taught at Rogers High School.

Elizabeth Meikle

The "house of black" undergoing renovation in 1949. The photograph above shows the ballroom being demolished and permanently removed.

Mary Healy was also a woman of independent means. She continued to live in the building when it became a full-fledged guest house. When Cozzens put the house up for sale in 1971, Healy bought it and turned Cliffside into the Cliffside Inn, a bed-and-breakfast establishment. The property changed hands again in 1981, when the Cliffside Inn was acquired by Mrs. Kathleen "Kay" Russell of Newport.

A number of Beatrice Turner paintings had been left hanging on the walls of Cliffside when the "loose" canvasses were cleaned out and carted off to the dump in 1948—in twelve truckloads, according to the Nathan Fleischer lecture. The haunting 1921 dual portrait of Beatrice and her mother had survived all the changes of ownership, and was prominently displayed in the parlor of the Cliffside Inn when Win Baker arrived to audition the place in 1989. "That painting was the strongest single impression I had about the building the first day I saw it, and, in fact, it outweighed everything else by a great margin," Baker said. "It was the single most attractive and interesting thing about the house, in the house or out of the house." The same painting was in the same place eight years earlier when Kay Russell first visited Cliffside, and it had the same effect on her. The first question Mrs. Russell asked then-owner Mary Healy was, "Does the painting come with the house?"

Kay Russell

Beatrice-fascination can be infectious. Kay Russell, who continues to wonder if Beatrice might have been a victim of child abuse, had made three substantial contributions to Turner lore during her stewardship of Cliffside. She contacted John Hopf and obtained from him a copy of the audiocassette on which Hopf had preserved the Nathan Fleischer recording. She found at a flea market in New York City a copy of the July 10, 1950 issue of *LIFE* magazine—the issue with the photospread of Turner paintings. And she purchased at a local auction in Newport the only three volumes of the Turner diaries currently known to exist.

All of this material was eventually made available to Win Baker. An extremely imaginative and creative man, Baker had made a career of seeing possibilities that other people didn't see, of being the "right person at the right time." At Westinghouse in the early 1960s, he worked with Mike Wallace on two programs that have never been duplicated: *Close-Up USA*, an intimate portrait of America, for which Wallace hit the road and conducted interviews in each of the fifty states, and *P.M. East . . . P.M. West*, an innovative late-night program broadcast simultaneously from New York and San Francisco. Baker was a member of the program staff of Westinghouse's next late-night entry, the legendary, freewheeling *Steve Allen Show*, the only syndicated talk show that ever seriously challenged *The Tonight Show Starring Johnny Carson*. Win Baker was one of the production executives that Westinghouse would bring in to fix programs that weren't working. He persuaded Merv Griffin to move his faltering late-night gab fest to an afternoon time slot, where it subsequently prospered, and was the first person to spot talk-show potential in an anchorwoman named Oprah Winfrey at WJZ-TV in Baltimore, and in Tom Snyder and Bill O'Reilly who were anchoring the news, respectively, at KYW-TV in Philadelphia and WNEV(TV) in Boston. All three eventually went on to national prominence because Baker created talk shows for them when they were working for him at local TV stations. Baker also created Westinghouse's innovative, nationally syndicated *PM Magazine* (1976), the much-praised forerunner of "reality TV." As an independent producer in the 1980s, he hired a San Francisco-based, black British psychiatrist, Dr. Loma Flowers, and put her on the air helping African-American patients cope with typical African-American problems. The show ran on Black Entertainment Television (BET) and was avidly followed by a large white and black audience. Flowers counselled AIDS victims, black and white, on camera during the earliest stages of the epidemic, when there was hardly any awareness of the disease outside of the gay community. These sessions received so much sympathetic interest that Baker went on to produce the first major PBS special on AIDS.

While working in San Francisco, Baker and one of the partners in his production company bought the Pillar Point Inn, a bed-and-breakfast in Princeton-by-the Sea, the only remaining fishing village between San Francisco and Monterey. Owning an inn proved to be something of an unexpected education, but Baker was a quick study. He decided to take the experience he had acquired at Pillar Point, which was subsequently sold to a group of Japanese businessmen, and apply it to a property close to his Connecticut home. When he walked into the Cliffside Inn, he walked into a Victorian manor house and a story, and the story, which he pieced together from the painting that came with the house, the Fleischer tape and the *LIFE* magazine article, suggested some extraordinary possibilities. Baker bought and refurbished the Cliffside Inn, and undertook the most extensive investigation into Beatrice Turner's life and work since Nathan Fleischer folded his tent in New England forty years earlier.

The first thing Baker did was to try to find Nathan Fleischer. When Fleischer left Newport, his collection of Turner art—the paintings Baker had seen in *LIFE* magazine—had seemingly disappeared with him. Fleischer seemed to be the key to the whereabouts of the paintings, and of course, Baker had no way of knowing that Fleischer had died just about the time Baker started looking for him. His sleuthing led to some of the most interesting people in Newport.

John Hopf had practically defined how visitors to Newport see Newport. His self-published, full-color picture books *The Complete Book of Newport Mansions*, *The Complete Picture Guide to Newport, R.I.* and *Newport Then and Now* are available all over Rhode Island, and are perennial bestsellers. In addition to being one of the best photographers in New England, Hopf is also a filmmaker, an award-winning telescope maker—he won a prize for optical excellence at the Amateur Telescope Makers Convention in Springfield, Vermont in 1965—a musician and a composer. For many years he wrote piano arrangements for silent movies screened at the old Casino Theatre in Newport and at the Newport Art Museum. He is also a gun collector, a Life Member of the National Rifle Association, a recipient of the N.R.A.'s Expert Rifleman award during his target shooting days, and a political activist—he was at one time president of the Newport Taxpayers Association and is presently the oldest member of that group's Board of Directors.

Hopf was recovering from a head injury when Baker got in touch with him. He had been in a coma, and when he regained consciousness he had lost his command of language. After months of speech therapy, he regained most

John Hopf has taken more than 3,000,000 photographs in, around and above Newport during his professional career spanning over 60 years.

of his vocabulary, but is still in the process of recovering his piano repertoire, which had ranged from Franz Liszt to Scott Joplin.

Hopf had a New York City address for Nathan Fleischer: Carnegie Hall. His information was correct, but it was twenty years out of date. There are 120 apartments in the Carnegie Hall complex. Leonard Bernstein occupied one of them in the 1940s, and Marlon Brando, Paddy Chayevsky and Martha Graham lived there in the 1950s. Nathan Fleischer was a tenant from 1963 to 1969, the period during which he attended graduate school at Yeshiva University and earned a Ph.D. Fleischer moved to Greenwich Village in 1970.

Hopf told Baker that, so far as he knew, Fleischer was in New York, at Carnegie Hall, doing P.R. work for Grossinger's. Tania Grossinger knew the Amazing Nathan as a kid growing up at Grossinger's and once tried past-life regression with him as an adult ("We tried. Unsuccessfully," she said). She denied that he ever had a public relations role with her family's resort. Fleischer apparently maintained some connection with Grossinger's during his Carnegie Hall period. His listing in the Manhattan white pages from 1963 to 1967 carried this additional line: "Fri Sat Sun Ask operator for Grossinger NY . . . Liberty 960." (Thereafter, he was listed as *Dr.* Nathan Fleischer.) Baker went to Carnegie Hall, but found no trace of Fleischer. Grossinger's was also a dead end; the resort had closed in 1985.

Baker then went to the Rhode Island Bar Association; Fleischer had been a lawyer before he became a psychologist and had practiced in Rhode Island. Another dead end. No one connected with the Rhode Island bar knew how to get in touch with Fleischer. About this time, Baker happened to read a column by Leonard Panaggio of the *Newport Daily News*. Panaggio seemed to know all there was to know about his native city. Baker had an inspiration and gave Panaggio a call. Leonard Panaggio had worked as a writer, editor and publicist, and has written and lectured on New England history. He is particularly fond of entertaining, off-beat historical anecdotes. He once wrote an hilarious essay for the *Bulletin of the Connecticut Historical Society* describing the enthusiastic reception given by the city of Hartford, Connecticut in 1842, when American naval vessels were a rarity in New England, for a training ship, the U.S. *Apprentice*, and its crew of forty teenage cadets. Panaggio is also an expert in using the media to disseminate information. He was the first director of public relations for Old Sturbridge Village in Massachusetts, and the first director of public relations for the State of Rhode Island. Panaggio's wife, Monique, who is French and who is also a writer, editor and publicist, was for forty years the public relations director of the Preservation Society of Newport County, the organization that maintains the Breakers, the Elms and numerous other mansions and historical buildings, and editor of the *Newport Gazette*, a quarterly publication of the Preservation Society. The Panaggios met in Casablanca, during World War II, where Leonard served with the U.S. Air Force. Ironically, the last two movies he saw before being shipped overseas were *Casablanca* and *Road to Morocco*.

Panaggio didn't know Nathan Fleischer, but did remember him as a political reformer in Newport. He was intrigued by the Beatrice Turner story and devoted a July, 1991 column to describing Win Baker's quest for leads on either Beatrice, Nathan or the Turner art works. The column attracted the at-

Beatrice Turner self-portrait "Through the Looking Glass" (1932).

*Leonard and Monique Panaggio at the time of their marriage
in Casablanca during World War II.*

tention of several people who either owned works of art by Beatrice Turner or
knew someone who did, including the Reverend Roy MacKaye Atwood of
Wethersfield, Connecticut, whose sister had posed for Beatrice, and Carol
Geary, the great-niece of Mrs. Elizabeth Meikle, the woman who purchased
Cliffside from the Turner estate. Ms. Geary, a Newporter, had two pencil
drawings, both Turner self-portraits, that had been found in the house after
Mrs. Meikle took possession. One is particularly striking. Beatrice sketched
it in Philadelphia in 1932, when she was in her early forties. She noted the
setting, 2322 Spruce Street, in a corner of the drawing, along with her signature, the date, and a title: "Through the Looking Glass." The picture captures
her reflection in a mirror on a raw, wintry day. Her hair is windblown, and
she's clutching the lapels of her wrap. She looks ravishing, lonely and receptive. The drawings were passed down through two generations of the Meikle
famiy.

The Panaggio column also led to Win Baker's meeting with Colonel
Hezekiah Ezekiel St. John. A Tennessee-born civil engineer, Zeke St. John

Carol Geary

served in three wars and with three different branches of the armed forces. He was in the navy during World War II, a civilian employee of the Air Force in Alaska during the Korean War, and a civilian advisor to the Marine Corps in Vietnam in 1966–67. He is a colonel (retired) in the Rhode Island State Militia. Zeke and Nathan Fleischer were great friends during Fleischer's Newport period.

Zeke was working for the Department of Agriculture, assisting New England farmers at the time. St. John was married in 1950, and Nat Fleischer was his best man. Zeke St. John was Nat Fleischer's right-hand man. When Fleischer was preparing to open the Turner exhibit at the Cliff Lawn Manor and wanted to attract attention, he sent Zeke to the Long Wharf to retrieve a skull that hung on the wall in one of the buildings along the waterfront; Zeke planted the skull in the broken concrete in the basement of Cliff Lawn where it would be found by workmen who were digging up the old floor and laying a

"Zeke" St. John (right) and best man Nathan Fleischer
at St. John's wedding (1950).

new one. This gave Fleischer what contemporary political consultants call "deniability." When the skull was unearthed and the police were summoned and the newspapers were called, Fleischer said, "I know nothing about it. My hands are clean."

On another occasion, Fleischer decided to burn Cliff Lawn to the ground to collect the insurance money, and Zeke was supposed to light the fire. Fleischer was stranded in Miami Beach at the time. He had spent all of his money driving to Miami Beach, with the Turner paintings in a trailer, and renting a storefront in town to exhibit the paintings, but the municipal authorities wouldn't allow the show to open. Fleischer had included a few nudes in his collection of Turner self-portraits, and these works, which are innocent enough by today's standards, were considered racy and pornographic in the Truman era. To make ends meet, Fleischer had gone to work for the Cole Brothers Circus, performing certain janitorial services for the Cole Brothers elephants. Out of desperation he had arranged with Zeke St. John to commit arson. Then he found out that the insurance policy on Cliff Lawn had *lapsed*. Fleischer tried to call St. John off, but there was a storm and the long-distance lines were down. Fortunately, Zeke never had the heart to go through with the plan in the first place.

Zeke had stayed in touch with Fleischer after Fleischer left Newport. He knew that Fleischer had never married and was able to tell Win Baker when and where Fleischer died. However, Zeke had no idea what happened to the Beatrice Turner paintings that Fleischer had exhibited in Newport and tried to exhibit in Miami Beach. Baker had dreamed of recovering the lost Turner paintings ever since he had seen pictures of them in *LIFE* magazine. He now had some wonderful Nathan Fleischer stories and had located a couple of extant Turner art works. But his chances of finding the Fleischer collection seemed to have died in California when Nat Fleischer lost his lifelong battle with diabetes in 1990.

Baker would not call it quits. If a large collection had disappeared, maybe a painting here and a painting there might materialize, and a small collection could be put together. Beatrice had been a resident of the Newport summer colony for two-thirds of her life; she died in Philadelphia during the summer of 1948, but had spent the previous forty consecutive summers, year in and year out, at Newport. Baker felt there might be—had to be—more Turner works in and around Newport, or at least more leads. On August 3, 1992, he took out an advertisement in the *Newport Daily News*. "WANTED: Anyone who owns or knows the whereabouts of paintings or drawings by BEATRICE TURNER, please call Mrs. Mede at 847-1811 about a 1993 benefit exhibition and videotape production of a permanent Turner Archive Collection."

Annette and Norbert Mede were an industrious, twenty-something couple Win Baker had hired at the time as the Cliffside innkeepers. The ad ran for a week; by the end of it, the Medes had received one call. It was from A. J. Sardella.

Beatrice Turner self–portrait (1924) at age 36.

VI

"I'll never forget when Norbie and Annette called me," Baker said. "A. J. had called Cliffside and said something like, 'I think you're asking in your ad about some paintings that we have. I'm not sure, but you're welcome to come and see them if you want to.' They went crazy when they went over there. They knew who Beatrice Turner was; they had read the *LIFE* magazine article and had heard the Nathan Fleischer tape. They were as stunned by what they saw as I was the first time I heard the tape. I think they thought, 'Well, who are these people, and maybe they have a painting. They said they had 'some.' It sounds unusual that they would have *some*, but, anyway, let's go over and see what they have.'

"I'll never forget when Norbie called me, because he said, 'You won't believe this. They're everywhere! They're everywhere! Some of them are little, and some of them are big. In their apartment, as you walk around the hallways, every time you turn a corner, or enter a room or even an alcove or a part of a room, there is one of these big paintings staring you right in the face.' And I remember he said, 'And here's the really surprising thing—they're not

Norbert and Annette Mede
(At Cliffside in 1992)

even in frames! They're all warped. They're just hung on the wall. They're not even in frames, they're just stretched canvasses, and they're old, and they're chipping.' He said, 'You won't believe it. I can't describe it. You have to go and see for yourself.'

"So I made an appointment right away to go and see them, and within a day I was up there." Norbert Mede had taken a camera with him to A. J. and Tony's and had photographed the paintings he had seen there. Baker saw the photographs before he went over to see A. J. and Tony. He knew that the paintings they had were part of the Fleischer collection, because he had seen a couple of those paintings in the 1950 *LIFE* photospread.

A. J. and Tony live within a ten-minute drive of the Cliffside Inn. "When I went in there," Baker said, "even though I knew I was going to see a lot of Beatrice Turner paintings, and even though I had already seen pictures of them, when I saw the real thing, it was a feeling I've only ever had, you know, a few times in my life. It was such excitement to find something like that. It was like finding buried treasure. I wanted to just grab them and take them all and run out of there. I couldn't believe what I was seeing. I mean, after all this time, all this talk, all these conversations, all these dead ends, all the searching for Nathan Fleischer, all of the above, here was the real thing, and it wasn't one of them or two of them, but fifteen or sixteen. Going there and seeing them for the first time was one of the most exciting moments I ever had in my whole life."

A. J. and Tony had six Turner self-portraits ranging from a dreamy-eyed, twenty-two-year-old Beatrice to a dashing Beatrice in her forties. They had two large dual portraits of Beatrice and her mother, Adele, which were painted fourteen years apart and are quite different in style, but equally impressive—a lively, impressionistic 1916 "crowd scene" showing the two women at the Newport Casino tennis courts and a smart, gorgeous 1930 "two shot" of the artist and her mother seated at a reception. They also had five portraits of Beatrice's mother, a portrait of her mother and father, and two still lifes.

An unexpected windfall. But a curious pattern began to emerge. Whenever Baker thought that all possibilities had been exhausted in the search for Turner art work and he had come to the end of the line, something unexpected *always* seemed to turn up. A hot tip brought Baker to Salas' Restaurant, a popular, family-owned eatery on Thames Street in Newport, which, in turn, led to meetings with members of the Salas family living outside of Newport, Jose Salas of Providence, Rhode Island, and his brother Rick, who lives and works in New York City. The brothers had three more paintings—two portraits of Adele and a Beatrice self-portrait; the latter was a smiling Beatrice in a festive blue hat. The pictures had apparently been picked up off the same pile on Rhode Island Avenue from which A. J. and Tony had salvaged their collection and could be directly traced to Nathan Fleischer's intervention at the 1948 bonfire. Like A. J. and Tony, the Salas brothers "didn't know who the 'lady in the hat' was" either.

Art work that Beatrice had given away or that had been acquired by other means began to surface too. Susan King of Middletown, Rhode Island had a stunning double portrait Beatrice had painted of her and a cousin, Seabury Brady, as children during the summer of 1945. Brady's father purchased the painting from the Turner estate after Beatrice's death. Newport artist Bettie Sarantos had a 1946 Beatrice Turner self-portrait, the most matronly Turner image rediscovered to date and perhaps one of the last self-portraits Beatrice ever painted. The people who owned the painting previously had taken it to Newport's oldest fine art gallery, Roger King Galleries on Bowen's Wharf, hoping that Roger King would sell it for them. Sarantos works at the King Galleries, liked the painting and bought it herself.

New York magazine gave the Cliffside Inn a complimentary write-up in its April 1992 spring travel issue and mentioned Beatrice Turner along with the breakfast menu, the draperies and the jacuzzis. In response, the Inn received a call from Joan Shand of Lancaster, Pennsylvania, who, as a young nurse, had taken care of Beatrice when she was dying of cancer in University Hospital in Philadelphia, and who had two portraits Beatrice had painted of her in appreciation of her kindness; these are the last works of art Beatrice was known to have completed.

Along about this time, Zeke St. John remembered something that Nathan Fleischer's other surviving Newport confidant, John Hopf, had forgotten. St. John had been following Win Baker's investigation with interest and remembered the paintings Baker described having seen at A. J. and Tony's. Zeke remembered seeing those paintings, almost half a century ago, spread out one at a time on a blanket on the manicured lawn of the Cliff Lawn Manor, while John Hopf stood over the paintings and took pictures of them. Hopf had made black-and-white photographs and some sixteen Kodachrome slides of the material Nathan had rescued. Fleischer had mailed a batch of prints to various newspapers and magazines to drum up publicity; this was how *LIFE* magazine and the *American Weekly* were induced to cover Nathan's 1949–50 exhibition.

The basement of John Hopf's house is divided into two large workspaces, one with photography equipment, the other with disc- and tape-recording equipment and a grand piano. The workspaces are also storage spaces. For 60 years, Hopf has photographed, filmed or recorded almost everything that took place in and around Newport that interested him. His entire life's work—60 years' worth of negatives, 16mm film, phonograph records and reels of tape—are packed in boxes or piled in stacks in these two basement rooms. Hopf may have a better collection of memorabilia than the Newport Historical Society. In one box or stack or another are large reels of Kodachrome movies of newsworthy events going back to the 1930s, including all of the America's Cup races in living memory up until 1983, when the United States lost the trophy to Australia.

Hopf made vinyl recordings of Nathan Fleischer's radio addresses during the mayoral campaigns of 1948 and 1950. The old records recently turned up in one box. You can hear the radio address in which Fleischer indicted the opposition; it was broadcast on October 29, 1948 and was entitled "Nathan Fleischer Prosecutes the Politicians." You can also hear Fleischer's forthright response on October 31, 1948 to the charges that were levelled against him—such as the charge that he was from Brooklyn. ("I'm from New York, I have lived in Brooklyn. I'm not ashamed of it," he said. "And both of my opponents, the Republican and Democratic candidates, were *born* in Brooklyn!")

At Baker's request, Hopf searched his archives, box by box, stack by stack, and—another windfall—found photographs and transparencies of some seventy paintings and drawings, including about three dozen works of art that presumably no longer exist. The lost Fleischer collection had survived more or less intact in photographic form.

Win Baker couldn't believe his eyes. "When John showed me what he had," Baker said, "it was another revelation that was so exciting. It was like going to Tony and A. J.'s, but in a different way. But it was the same sensation for me because here was a visual record of everything that was there. I saw all of the paintings that were in *LIFE* magazine. I saw paintings I had seen live at A. J. and Tony's apartment. Then I saw paintings I've never seen before in either place, and the combination was unbelievable to me."

Baker made sure that the Fleischer collection will stay found by documenting all of the rediscovered Turner images in a videotape he produced, *In Search of Beatrice Turner*. By late 1992, he had tracked down some 33 extant original works of art by Beatrice Turner. Beatrice's paintings have a bewitching attraction, particularly the self-portraits. She portrayed herself as a radiant, reserved, reflective woman who always seems to have noticed something gratifying—perhaps the attention of a man. Or perhaps, having entered a ball or reception, she is suddenly aware of having attracted everyone's admiring attention. In more casual settings, seated, for example, with her puppy on her knee, she seems gracious, discerning and aware. The images shimmer with personality, and the people who own them and live with them are remarkably attached to them.

Win Baker offered to buy the art works he had located, but neither A. J. and Tony nor any of the other owners were willing to sell. They did, however, allow him to gather all of the extant material in one place for a retrospective. "Remembering Beatrice Turner," the first public exhibition of Beatrice's work since Nathan Fleischer closed his show on the road in 1950, opened, appropriately enough, at the Cliffside Inn in January of 1993.

Interest was keen, both in Newport and in the media. Articles appeared in the *Providence Journal*, *Rhode Island Monthly*, the *Boston Globe*, *Country Inns* and *Art & Antiques*. ABC-TV's *Good Morning America* descended on the Cliffs and aired a sympathetic feature broadcasting the Beatrice legend and a

These three Beatrice Turner self-portraits were among some 70 photographs and transparencies taken in 1949 by John Hopf and found in his basement in 1992.

Most of Beatrice's work was destroyed in 1948 and because the majority of the surviving works are oils, there is no clear evidence of how she allocated her efforts among various art media. The variety of the 12 sketches that survive suggests she may have sketched as prolifically as she painted. The trove found in John Hopf's basement included the three sketches shown on this page.

The 110 surviving Turner art images include these four unusual works, which were actually self-portraits in disguise. Beatrice created paintings of statuette busts with variations of her own face worked into the design.

selection of her stunning self-portraits to a national audience. Again the curious pattern repeated itself: whenever the tale of Beatrice and Baker's search for her art work received any kind of publicity, more paintings inevitably turned up. This time Baker received two calls. One was from J. William Winter of Oriental, North Carolina, a retired print production manager in the advertising business. Bill Winter's mother, the late Edna May Haley Winter, and Beatrice Turner had been classmates at the Pennsylvania Academy of the Fine Arts, and fellow members of the Plastic Club, the Philadelphia women's art group. Beatrice had given Mrs. Winter three original works of art, and Bill Winter had one of them: a portrait of a nude woman who can't be positively identified because she's hiding her face. The other two works were still lifes. They were owned by Bill Winter's late brother David, and had passed into the possession of David's daughter, Cheryl Winter.

The second caller was Peppi Mishcon, a divorcée living in North Miami Beach. Mrs. Mishcon had formerly lived on Long Island in southeastern New York, and had met Nathan Fleischer at Grossinger's in the mid-1950s when Nathan was performing as a hypnotist, putting people to sleep and making them cluck like chickens, and so on. She was married then, and she and her ex-husband and their friends were a lively group, and Nathan had played to them. After the performance, she asked Nathan if he would come down to Long Island and perform at one of her parties. He said he'd be delighted to. A month or two later, he put people to sleep and made them cluck like chickens in her living room in Belle Harbor.

A few weeks later, Nathan called and asked Mrs. Mishcon if he could use her living room for a hypnosis demonstration. He had rented a small room in a temple somewhere and was expecting about twenty doctors or dentists, but the doctors or dentists were bringing their wives and he needed more space. Mrs. Mishcon wasn't planning to be home anyway at the day and time when Nathan needed the space, so she readily agreed. Sometime later, Nathan stopped by the house—Mrs. Mishcon was out—and left two items with the maid to express his gratitude: a copy of the July 10, 1950 issue of *LIFE* magazine and a 1923 Beatrice Turner self-portrait. "I was overwhelmed," Mrs. Mishcon said. "When I moved from Long Island to Florida, I got rid of everything but that painting. And I told my children, 'Don't sell that painting when I kick off.'"

The self-portrait was one of the works John Hopf had photographed and happened to be Win Baker's favorite of all of the Turner material documented by Hopf. It is a remarkable composition and a striking contrast to the "belle of the ball" motif of almost all the other self-portraits. Beatrice was 35 years old in 1923, but she looks several years younger on this canvas and hauntingly beautiful. She wears an enormous picture hat piled with plumes and decorations, and a frilly, low-cut dress. She's also wearing a jaunty pair of earrings—two large pearls dangling from each ear. Only her head and shoulders are visible. She's staring straight ahead, her face and neck bathed in a fiery sunset glow. She seems to have taken an uncertain step forward, arriving at a mysterious destination perhaps unexpected and unannounced. In Joseph Campbell's phrase, she certainly seems to have "followed her bliss," and to have done so bravely. She seems to have summoned all of her will to give herself so freely, and now stands between daylight and darkness, awaiting what the very next moment will bring, appearing astonishingly vulnerable, innocent and open. What is she seeing? What is she looking for?

Every extant image that can be identified as having been painted or drawn by Beatrice Turner, or even sketched in her diary, is now permanently exhibited at the Cliffside Inn. A few are originals; most are reproductions, including laser digital reproductions of A. J. Sardella and Tony Vasak's beloved warped and chipping canvasses, and blow-ups of the missing and presumed lost material photographed in color or black-and-white by John Hopf. Every room is decorated with a different set of Turner compositions. A reproduction of the flaming self-portrait is prominently displayed in the parlor at Cliffside, the place where guests congregate and breakfast and tea are served. It invariably galvanizes everyone's attention.

The rich, warm, vibrant, delectably Victorian interiors of the inn seem to magically evoke the spirit of the talented "Century Lady" who lived and worked there in a more innocent age. Cliffside is generally considered Newport's most popular romantic hideaway. Many of the thousands of people from around the country who visit the inn each year and see the paintings in the house where most, if not all, of them were painted have become Win Baker's "stringers," scouting their localities for more Turner art work. As of this writing, a total of 41 existing works of art by Beatrice Turner have been catalogued by Baker: 29 oil paintings, five watercolors, and seven drawings. Numbers 40 and 41 are particularly interesting.

Number 40, a 1926 dual portrait of Beatrice and Adele Turner, was spotted at a roadside sale near Flemington, New Jersey by one of Baker's "scouts," Jonathan Ridge Fell, a computer executive who regularly stays at the Cliffside Inn when in Newport. It is perhaps the most handsome dual portrait Beatrice ever painted of herself and her mother, and is a particularly significant find because this painting wasn't in *LIFE* magazine, wasn't photographed by Hopf and therefore almost certainly was not part of the collection Nathan Fleischer had salvaged from the Newport fire. Twelve truckloads of Turner art reportedly went up in flames in Newport in 1948. Beatrice's primary residence, however, was in Philadelphia, and some large number of her artistic compositions were created, stored and displayed there. This is not supposition: a copy of her will surfaced in Newport in March of 1997. In this document, she names six women and requests "that each of these be empowered to select a painting by my mother or by myself in my house, 2322 Spruce Street, Philadelphia, or at my house, "Cliffside," Newport, Rhode Island, in memory of their friendship." The Turner estate was sold at auction in Philadelphia in 1949 by Samuel T. Freeman and Company, now Freeman Fine Arts of Philadelphia, Inc., the oldest auction house in America. The firm can find no record of sales of Turner paintings and no longer has the original auction contract, which would have included an inventory of the estate. How many paintings Beatrice may have given away in her lifetime, how many paintings may have been found in her Philadelphia townhouse after her death, how many of these may have been salvaged, how many other "undiscovered" Turner paintings may be gathering dust in closets, attics, garages or storerooms in Philadelphia or Newport or anywhere else is anyone's guess.

Extant art work number 41 was located during this writing as a result of one of the bequests Beatrice made in her will. It is a 1927 portrait of Mrs. Charles Roberts, a philanthropist and former president of the Pennsylvania Society of the Colonial Dames of America. It was found in the Common Room of Founders Hall of Haverford College in Haverford, Pennsylvania, the only portrait of a woman in a gallery of portraits of male founders, educators and board members of the college. The Roberts portrait is a most significant discovery because it tells us a couple of things about Beatrice Turner that Nathan Fleischer and *LIFE* magazine didn't: she was a serious artist, and she didn't live in a dream world.

This large dual portrait was found by a Cliffside Inn guest on his way home from Newport at a yard sale in New Jersey.

This Turner portrait of Philadelphia philanthropist Mrs. Charles Roberts hangs in the Common Room of Founder's Hall at Haverford College in Pennsylvania.

Beatrice Turner self–portrait sketch (1928) at age 40.

VII

*I*f Beatrice started keeping her diary at the age of 18 and continued right up until her death, then she wrote for 42 years and made a total of 15,330 daily entries. She wrote in a fine, graceful, unostentatious hand—no frilly embroidery—and illustrated the diary here and there with evocative sketches. Typical entries vary in length from half a page to two or more pages. Based on the most reasonable and conservative assumptions, the mathematics works out this way: she may have easily compiled a *minimum* of 25 to 30 thousand pages in her lifetime. As with her paintings and drawings, however, only a small portion of the diary survives: a couple of entries that were part of the Nathan Fleischer exhibition and which John Hopf had photographed for his files, and the sections purchased at auction by Kay Russell, the woman who sold the Cliffside Inn to Win Baker in 1989. Mrs. Russell's material covers a period of 101 days, from June 19 through September 28, 1927, when Beatrice was 39, and another 88 days, from March 11 through June 6, 1935, when she was 47. Hopf's photographed pages—those that are dated—are from 1920, when Beatrice was 32, and from 1941

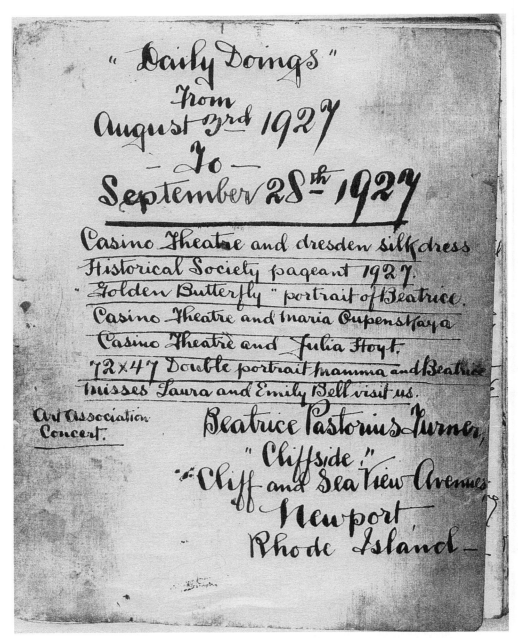

"Daily Doings"
from
August 3rd 1927
To
September 28th 1927

Casino Theatre and dresden silk dress
Historical Society pageant 1927.
"Golden Butterfly" portrait of Beatrice.
Casino Theatre and maria Oupenskaya
Casino Theatre and Julia Hoyt.
72×47 Double portrait mamma and Beatrice
misses Laura and Emily Bell visit us.

Art Association
Concert.

Beatrice Pastorius Turner,
"Cliffside,"
Cliff and Sea View Avenues
Newport,
Rhode Island —

Beatrice's diaries were entitled "Daily Doings". This page is typical of the way in which specific time periods were labeled and separated.

and 1942, when she was 53 and 54. The Hopf and Russell finds combined add up to a total of some 201 pages, or less than one percent of the projected total.

The mysteries that arise when one first encounters the Beatrice story are not dispelled in these pages. She doesn't explain why she painted all those self-portraits and wore the Victorian clothes, or why she didn't marry or travel or try, in some substantial way, to market her talents as a portraitist and illustrator. There are no definitive answers or telltale clues. Two hundred and one pages representing a few days, weeks or months of each of five years of the life of an enigmatic woman who lived almost 60 years is not a large enough sample to settle an investigation of her life and times.

Of course, smallness is itself relative. One minute cell plucked from a single hair follicle contains within its nucleus the virtual library of genetic information that sets each of us apart from all other human beings on this multitudinous planet, and from which our individual life histories, in biological terms, can be reconstructed. Similarly, Beatrice exists on every one of those 201 pages. She invested a part of herself in every page she wrote—her thoughts, feelings, interests. In this sense, the surviving microcosm of her diaries provides an enormous amount of information about her, so that when you focus in, so to speak, a real person, a real life emerges.

And it's a revelation.

The real Beatrice was a woman of depth and taste, a woman who was very much aware of the world around her, and who had so much poetry in her soul that she seems to have been effortlessly able to paint marvelously evocative word-pictures of the settings in which she moved. Images that writers grasp for seem to have flown freely from her pen:

> Still very cold. Furnace going! Ice on the back-kitchen roof of the house next door. Snow in slim dropped bursts blown horizontally about the streets.

> Lovely in the twilight. The velvety softness of lawns and deep greens on the great old trees. The lovely desertion and the perfect

The sketches on these two pages are montages of drawings taken from the pages of Beatrice's diaries. The more elaborate drawing (upper left) depicts an opera Beatrice reviewed in her diary. The others are "people watching" impressions at Newport events Beatrice attended.

given to the head, which needs it when brushed down teeth and added to (*This*) *fashion — very heavy rotund Egypt's effect.*

*2nd)
ly daring in dialogue
ras clever + quick
red not at all
A young French woman
on, goodlooking,
ly a gambler
re, a room leading
m of a gambling
The young
ppearance
lemon
de style
s at
ld her
t leave
asino*

*rain bow depth of color
Mable*

* us
ftion
to us*

*hame
so in*

The drawings on the right side of this page reflect Beatrice's continuing interest in the then current fashions of Newport high society. The drawing at top left shows Beatrice and her mother leaving a reception in Philadelphia. The sketch at bottom left accompanied a diary description of a rainbow that broke through dark clouds after a violent Newport storm.

flowers and the tree-hidden houses. Hardly a disillusioning motor car. No pedestrians. Calmness. Peace.

Casual descriptions, the first of a late winter's day in Philadelphia, the second of a Newport by-road, but the writing is so vivid, fresh, resonant and succinct that the reader is immediately pulled right into the scene. You can almost see the bootprints of your own galoshes in the half-inch of snow that must have accumulated on those streets. You can almost hear a leaf drop on that deserted by-road. Here she is in her wildflower garden at Cliffside:

> Sweet William and Canterbury bells in fullest and luscious bloom, a blaze of color! The Canterbury bells are particularly magnificent. I have never before seen so many in flower at once anywhere. With the brighter color of the sweet William backing them they are truly exquisite, and when the winds sway them one listens for bells tingling from faery-land.

The last sentence is inspired. Since we associate the sound of a ringing bell with the sight of a bell in gently rocking motion, the "tingling" one is urged to listen for immediately brings home the visual image of what the Canterbury bells look like in full bloom "when the winds sway them." We can see in our minds exactly what Beatrice saw, exactly the way she saw it. Notice how she plays with sight, sound and texture in the following Newport passage. She was probably sitting by a window up on the third floor of Cliffside when she wrote it:

> A wonderful silvery rain, heavy and veiling, deepening all the greens of the foilage to lacquered lusciousness and playing its merry little tune on the great extent of our porch's tin roof—
> Ruffling the gray surface of the ocean with tiny white-capped waves and obscuring the details of the St. George's School tower

and its surrounding little English village on Easton's Point to Whistlerian harmonies—

And through it all, the distant, mournful query of the harbor's foghorns: "Who oo, who oo?"

The poetic sensibility the diaries reveal is as extraordinary as it is unexpected, and it's so completely unexpected as to be astonishing. Beatrice wasn't *supposed* to be a poet at heart. After all, as Win Baker puts it, "During her life, she was scorned by Newport society as a mysterious eccentric. After her death, she was reviled by the media as a tragic narcissist recluse." A woman accused of having been a victim of something that sounds as perverse as "egosexia" would hardly have been expected to have written this meditation on the tales of Hans Christian Andersen, after having read his autobiography:

> From "The Little Mermaid" to "The Snow Queen" and "The Chinese Emperor and the Nightingale"—how part of me they were, these dainty whimsies drawn with a touch as light and a pattern as precise and florescent as frost upon a window pane.
>
> One who has read them in youth will always be reminded of their fairy-winged lessons in odd moments throughout one's existence.
>
> Of childlike simplicity of thought and expression, they reach to one's inner life as no redundantly worded, high-flying work does— and gently one absorbs and their beauty becomes part of one.
>
> And these little miracles of tales were written by an oddly attractive, homely old man who all his life strove with singleness of intent to be somebody.
>
> Poor swanlet!

This isn't the Beatrice of the tale told by Nathan Fleischer from behind the dark draperies, the gothic tale disseminated in print by the *American Weekly* and *LIFE* magazine. This is Beatrice without the draperies. There are no traces of madness in these pages. Sadness, perhaps. "All my life I have done just what my family wished me," she wrote. And elsewhere: "I am leading a life I did not choose."

The world, she said, "adopts an 'Oh, aren't you married yet?' attitude," and she felt "condemned and snubbed." But moments of self-reflection and self-indulgence are notably few. Beatrice rarely unfolds; she was too well-bred. She doesn't apologize or accuse, exact vengeance or attempt to justify herself. She doesn't dwell on herself, her moods or resentments, nor does she draw much of a word-picture of the person who dominated most of her adult life: her mother.

Interestingly, when Beatrice painted her mother's portrait, or dual portraits of herself and Mama, she almost always portrayed her mother in profile. Full frontals of Adele Turner in her silver-haired maturity are practically nonexistent. We don't meet Mama "head-on" in the diaries either; she remains a peripheral figure, and psychologists, amateur and professional, can make of that what they will.

Beatrice entitled her diaries "Daily Doings," and they are just that, an almost journalistic account of what a highly intelligent and cultivated woman did, and what she saw and heard, in the high society days of Newport and Philadelphia. She read voraciously—she was something of a speed reader, apparently. She read the *New York Times*, the *Philadelphia Evening-Bulletin*, the *Philadelphia Record*, the *Newport Herald*, the *Saturday Evening Post*. She read novels, histories, biographies. She read aloud at times. ("More amusing as read aloud," she said of a contemporary novel.) She tended her garden. She worked on her art. ("What so voluptuous a sensation as a thoroughly dried canvas, almost finished, to be entirely repainted and altered!") And she went—with Mama—to the theatre, concerts, lectures.

When she looked at her surroundings, she saw light and color with an artist's eye, and painted luminous word-pictures of lingering sunsets. When she looked at what people, prominent and otherwise, said and did, she cast a discerning eye at the sound and fury, and saw at a glance exactly what it signified. "Saturday, William H. Vanderbilt's first wife, the former Emily Davies, committed suicide," Beatrice wrote in Philadelphia, on May 28, 1935.

Her eyesight was impaired, and she left a note saying that she did it because her child (a daughter) was not allowed to be with her. She had had a somewhat hectic career. Still, when, after a family spat, this daughter of a former partner of J. P. Morgan left Newport without bothering to take her baby, it was held that she had forfeited all right to the child by the politically powerful—and quite ruthless—Mrs. Ellen French Vanderbilt Fitz Simons, William's mother.

"Now, in Monday's *Newport Herald*, which we received in the mail today," Beatrice observed, "there is no word of the former Mrs. Vanderbilt's suicide." There was, however, a social note from Marienbad announcing that the second Mrs. William Vanderbilt had just had another operation. The implicit message?

Newporters, please sympathize with current wife!

Beatrice had a marvelous wit and was often hugely entertaining:

Of a passionate make-out party staged by a strapping maid and her soldier boyfriend in the back yard of the townhouse next door in Philadelphia—and in full view of the Turner sitting-room window—Beatrice said, "It was a riot. At times it was so energetic one could not be certain if it was an amatory or a pugilistic affair."

On a rare excursion to the movies, to see *The Scarlet Pimpernel*, Hollywood's romantic adventure of the French Revolution, she said, "The aristocrats in the prison scene—save for their fine clothes—look uncommonly like the jailors! If they were unable to secure more rarefied types, surely they might have had coarser ones for the attendants."

When a revamped edition of the *Pennsylvania Magazine of History and Biography*, a quarterly publication of the Historical Society of Pennsylvania, arrived in the mail, she reported that "The format has been changed (after 50 years) and there are no more illustrations. Three articles appear by three 'educators.' Pronounce it like Mrs. Lingelbach—open the mouth wide, push forth

*For perplexing, but unknown reasons, Beatrice almost never portrayed her
mother Adele full face or head–on, but rather in profile.*

In the 19 surviving art works which feature her mother, including the double portraits, Adele Tull Haas Turner's full face can be seen in only three.

the tongue and say lingeringly: *Edd-youu-kate-toors*. These consisting of a Pittsburgh high-school teacher and instructors at Wellesley College and M.I.T. I thought it was a magazine for *historians!*" (Anna Lane Lingelbach, a member of the Historical Society, was the first woman to serve on the Philadelphia Board of Education.)

There are some Turner mysteries that the diaries, if anything, deepen. Although Beatrice never changed with the times in a fashion sense, she was no hidebound traditionalist. She loved the performing arts and as a theater- and concertgoer was open-minded and receptive to innovation. When Isadora Duncan died, Beatrice wrote:

> I never saw her. She was very "new" in her day, believed in a woman's right to have children sans marriage rites and had three by no known father. A nursemaid carelessly let the perambulator containing them slide down an embankment in a Paris park, and Isadora's three experiments were drowned in the pond below. It was tragic, but moralists and sermonizers rather enjoyed it at the time.

In 1927, the French piano virtuoso Paul Doguereau, then an eighteen-year-old prodigy, gave a recital in Newport. The *Herald* criticized him for "an apparent love for the bizarre in piano music and a great affection for abrupt contrasts of sharp crashes and delicate passages." Beatrice didn't frown at the pyrotechnics. His vigorous interpretations, she wrote, were "very like improvization."

> It was enjoyable—as music always is in semi-darkness.

Doguereau would become the teacher of another charismatic stylist, Earl Wild, the first concert pianist to give a recital on American television.

Actress Julia Hoyt also performed in Newport in 1927. Hoyt was very much ahead of her time, both physically and theatrically. She was a tall, slender, elongated woman, a type unrepresented in the media three generations before the advent of Cindy Crawford. She starred in a Newport production of Molnar's classic bedroom farce, *The Guardsman*, racy entertainment for 1927, and wore on stage the kind of tight, formfitting, see-through gowns that Marlene Dietrich would squeeze into for her nightclub act in the 1950s and 1960s. "She was gorgeous," Beatrice wrote. *"A new design of a woman!"*

> And, to all intents, quite nude in each costume she wore. Every muscle was visible. A 20th century Venus. Her slenderness of hip in such a large woman I have never seen equalled, and how she managed to get the clothes to stick to her, unless there was glue in their composition, I cannot imagine. Nor have I ever, out of an artists' life class, seen more of a *display*. But she is beautiful of figure, and, if rather "squashed" of face, she had beautiful eyebrows and a very white skin for her black hair. Her shadows are translucent.

Her shadows are translucent. Was a more memorable line ever written in tribute to a performing artist? The Newport Casino Theatre, however, was in a state of shock.

> The audience was even colder than on former nights, and not a curtain call nor a flower came to the handsome star.

"She waited in the dressing room at the close of the performance for congratulations and congratulators who did not appear," Beatrice said. Two of the leading members of the summer colony, composer Shafter Howard and Dr. Stephen B. Luce "ran through the crowd crosswise to meet her."

> I should have liked to, *but*—

Beatrice's views often seemed to be at odds with prevailing opinion. On an overcast day in July of 1927, plans were approved for the restoration of

In 1927 Beatrice wrote (and sketched) admiringly in her diary of actress/socialite Julia Hoyt, as a "new design of a woman". Beatrice had seen Hoyt the previous evening in Molnar's "The Guardsman" at the Newport Casino theater.

Tuesday, August 23rd 1927
(continued 3rd)

Mrs H. Fish Webster and Mrs Robert Potter, Ruth Thomas, Mrs Glyn
The play — A Molnar Viennese translation — Very Viennese —
"The Guardsman". An actress, married to an actor is bored to
extinction — He impersonates a Prince, Russian, in General's
uniform — and courts his wife —
The actress — Julia Robins (Mrs Lydig Hoyt) Julia Hoyt —
This "social" New York beauty — at one time reported engaged
to Hermann Oelrichs — Very tall, very ~~slim~~ slim of hip
and waist, and broad of shoulder, with long and heavy
muscular neck of ivory white — She was gorgeous —
A new design of a woman! And, to all intents quite
nude in each costume she wore — Every ~~n~~
was visible — A 20th Century
of hip in such a large woman
equalled, and how ~~th~~ she
to stick to her unless there
I cannot imagine — nor ha
life class —, seen more of a
beautiful of figure, and if
she has beautiful eye **brows**,
for her black hair — Her shadows are translucent —

Newport's historic Trinity Church, a colonial landmark. The church fathers, like the music critic of the *Newport Herald*, emphasized authenticity over creativity. The plans called for a wine glass pulpit and the replacement of a late-nineteenth century stained glass window with a clear window. The window that was to be replaced was a creation of John La Farge (1835–1910), an American master of stained glass design. "Of course the window *is* an anachronism," Beatrice wrote.

> But it is inspiringly beautiful, a work of genius with a magnificence of color unsurpassed. (Oh, throw a hammer at it and be done with it!) Far more artistic to have a restoration of a plain church, of some beauty of line, unrelieved by the alien fire of this marvelously beautiful thing.
>
> Truly the minister may well orate from a "wine glass pulpit," and were the trustees to be placed back of him in cages the symbolism would be complete.

In short, she was an interesting woman with a mind of her own. She wrote poetry—she mentions writing verse in one diary entry, but didn't include the poem. She wrote a 210-page manuscript titled "1775." She mentions in her diary that she was working on this project, and she mentions having finished a rewrite. It's not clear whether this was a work of fiction or non-fiction, and there's no record of its having been published, or any indication whatsoever of what happened to the manuscript after she finished it. How much writing she did apart from the diary is still another Beatrice mystery. This one is impossible to solve because ninety-nine percent of "Daily Doings," the record of her adult life, is missing.

It's tragic that not more of the diary itself has survived. Beatrice Turner was writing about some of the most elevated and influential people in American history, gathered at a legendary place, at an extravagant time. If we had all or even half or at least a quarter of the diaries, we would have a stunning, eyewitness account of a fabulous era, told from a unique point of view. The loss is distressing. The longest section of the extant one percent of diary entries covers no more than one season of one year of Beatrice's life. Fortunately, it's the right season: summer. The summer of 1927, one of the last golden summers in a grand, gilded and glaringly supercilious Newport.

Beatrice Turner self–portrait (1931) at age 43.

VIII

The journey from Philadelphia to Newport was long and arduous in the first half of the twentieth century; it was accomplished by rail and sea, and took almost an entire day—a full 24 hours—to complete. In late spring of each year, Beatrice and her mother got on an early morning train at Reading Terminal in east Philadelphia and got off the train at midday in Jersey City, then the largest railhead in the eastern U.S. At Exchange Place in Jersey City, directly across the Hudson River from the financial district in New York, they boarded one of the Tuscan red ferryboats operated by the Pennsylvania Railroad. The ferry docked at Cortlandt Street in Lower Manhattan, where the marina and esplanade of the World Financial Center are located today. From Cortlandt Street, the Turners took a taxi to Pier 14, then at Fulton Street, to board the S.S. *Commonwealth*, the white-hulled flagship of the famous Fall River Line.

A phonograph or radio could be heard playing in the main entrance hall, someone singing opera magnificently. The open win-

The Turners spent winters in their Philadelphia townhouse at 2322 Spruce Street.

dow of our stateroom gave a magnificent view of New York's today, rather dingy skyline. Read newspapers and the *Saturday Evening Post*, which I went down to the boat-shed to buy.

The steamer *Commonwealth* was as luxuriously-appointed as the ships then plying the Atlantic and Pacific oceans. It departed New York late in the afternoon and arrived at the Long Wharf in Newport in the wee hours of the following day. By the time Beatrice unlocked the double-doors of Cliff-side, it would be almost dawn. In this instance, there was evidence of vandalism, the storm doors having been forced off their hinges and wrenched to one side.

I walked about the house to observe from outside if it had been broken into elsewhere. Apparently not. All in order. Now full daylight. Weigela in full and luscious bloom; wisteria in long, drooping flowers, but not as profuse as I have seen it. Went upstairs, opened up front bedroom window and put away furs.

Beatrice described the extent of the damage in her diary using words and pictures. The dialogue that later ensued with the policeman on the beat, which she carefully recorded, is priceless.

Casey, the Bellevue Avenue policeman said that he comes down here every day, all winter long.

I said, "Yes, I know you do, Mr. Casey, and when did you discover the door?" He looked sort of cross-eyed. And I said: "When were you down here *last?*"

He looked even more cross-eyed. "I'm down here every day," said Casey, "and I come up here on this porch every time. It must have been the wind that did it!"

Said I: "How could the *wind* do it?"

"Oh, there's terrible winds down here sometimes," said Casey. "Why, look at all the shingles what were blown off your roof! They blew off a long time ago. See, the grass has grown through them!"

as water will not come at once, Wegelia in full and lucious bloom — wistaria in long drooping flowers but not profuse as I have seen it. Belated situation. At all events off that awful gambling ship intact — m. & I and nothing gone from the house but doors wrenched forcibly from staples & from their & bolt of iron in center but not opened. And the endless enormously heavy as it is, bent screws & hooks at bottom anchoring doors to door sill from the inside are intact.

Beatrice illustrated her diary entry about the apparent vandalism in Newport.

But, Beatrice observed, "these were not shingles, but the tops of the battlements at the sides of the steps which were wantonly ripped off, the nails left standing up, and the light boards ripped to pieces and lying back of the hollyhocks." Officer Casey "became very vociferous and sought to make a great point of no instrument marks being visible on the door."

"Do you see any?" he asked.

"No," said I, "but I don't see what that has to do with it."

"It can't be criminal *if there's no marks*," stated Casey, appearing more cross-eyed than ever. "You don't consider this *burglary*, do you?" he asked, concerning the boards ripped off the battlements at the sides of the steps.

"No," said I, "I would call that a case of *malicious mischief*."

I do not know if he had ever heard the words before, but he nearly fell off the steps with chagrin. He subsided until Mama came out, whereupon he told her that she was "as popular as the Vanderbilts"!!!

A wave of innovation had transformed rural, isolationist, nineteenth-century America into a bustling world power. Enormous wealth had been created in the process, and Newport was its physical manifestation. In 1927, the upswing of the economic growth curve was still ascending. The major emphasis along palatial Bellevue Avenue and its adjuncts remained money and genealogy. The results often sounded like a page out of P. G. Wodehouse.

Out on grounds in late afternoon, transplanting balsam. Dr. George Bolling Lee, who rents the cottage opposite, was shouting, "You're an Indian, don't forget you're an Indian. You mustn't mind it," to the two youngsters, offspring of his decidedly November marriage to Miss Helen Keeney of July vintage. The Bollings are descended from Pocahontas, and apparently the children were being reminded of the redskin in the blood!

The real Pocahontas, as opposed to the Disney version, converted to Christianity, changed her name to Rebecca, and married Virginia colonist

John Rolfe, a tobacco planter. The couple had one child, a son. Dr. Lee, a Manhattan physician, was also a descendant of Robert E. Lee and "Lighthorse Harry" Lee, the Revolutionary War hero. (Additional Turner diaries might have indicated whether the Bolling Lees were prudent enough not to remind the children of the rebel in the blood.)

A wave of immigration would transform American life and the American elite, and, ironically, that wave crested at the very moment the Newport aristocracy was at the height of its glittering influence. As a result, ancestry lost its cachet. In the 1920s, however, a certain number of old, established families, connected by marriage ties, had been so well represented in leadership positions in government, business and the professions for generation after generation that bloodlines *meant* power. Genealogy *was* money. The Newport dynasties were no less Machiavellian in their exercise of power than the European houses they sought to emulate. ("Newport," according to a contemporary observer, New York City newspaperman Stanley Walker, was "known for its feuds, its cliques and its almost terrifying rudeness.") The rules of acceptance were rigidly enforced.

"Met Mrs. Elliott walking with her great-niece, a rather pretty blonde girl," Beatrice wrote in a painfully terse entry. She and her mother were strolling up beautiful Old Beach Road on their way home from a meeting at the Historical Society of Newport.

> Mrs. Elliott is no longer even politely disguising her viciousness to us.

Maud Howe Elliott, a recurring name in the diary and the embodiment of a recurring theme—exclusion—was Newport's leading literary and cultural light, and a founder of the Art Association of Newport. Mrs. Elliott was the author of numerous books about her famous and influential relatives, including her mother, abolitionist Julia Ward Howe, author of "The Battle Hymn of the Republic." Beatrice Turner wasn't taken seriously as an artist by the Art Association in 1927, and often mischievously referred to the organization as the "Art Assassination."

Out in afternoon with Mama to the Art Assassination for a reception for the incoming class at the Naval War College. Mrs. Elliott headed the receiving line. Mrs. (Admiral) Sims was second. She did not actually *refuse* to shake hands, but came close to it. Mrs. Eppley, third in line, practically *did* refuse. But I fixed her mit my basilisk eye, and she decided to behave.

Admiral William W. Sims was commander-in-chief of American naval forces in European waters during World War I. Mrs. Sims, the former Anne Hitchcock, was the daughter of Ethan Allen Hitchcock, who had served as Secretary of the Interior under Presidents McKinley and Roosevelt. Mrs. Marion Eppley, the former Ethelberta Pyne Russell, the woman on whom Beatrice fixed her basilisk eye, was a member of the Colonial Dames through 28 different ancestors, including a signer of the Declaration of Independence and a general of the Continental Army. (As a child, Mrs. Eppley had even had a socially correct pet: her dog was a descendant of a staghound owned by Sir Walter Scott, a distant cousin.)

"Intrigue and deviltry surround one from all sides," Beatrice had written seven years earlier, at the age of 32.

From the Casino to the Art Association, Red Cross Avenue to Merton Road, all seems a vicious interweaving of a swarm of malignant wasps, whirling their little lives of purposeless stinging in an ever fighting, flying vortex of ugly-minded black insect life.

It was difficult not to get stung. Two ancient and influential members of the Colonial Dames, the sisters Laura and Emily Bell of Philadelphia, visited Newport in the summer of 1927. Three days after reading of their arrival, in a social note in the *Herald*, Adele Turner collared the sisters in downtown Newport and brought them back to Cliffside for tea. This was quite a coup, considering that the Bells had previously been entertained by Mrs. J. Bertram Lippincott, the wife of the prominent Philadelphia publisher.

Miss Emily is fat and rather good-natured, with child-like blue eyes; Miss Laura, very thin, very prim, somewhat sour.

They came in and inspected the house and the pictures, all being, fortunately, in excellent order.

The house and grounds passed muster. "All was perfect," sighed Beatrice, "save Beatrice, who had on her old sateen paint coat and skirt."

They wanted to know if the furniture came from auction up here. (They were over lunching at Mrs. Bertram Lippincott's, suffice it to say.)

I assured them it did not. Only some of the frames came from auction in town.

Did we have the *whole* house?

Well, naturally.

On the whole they were not more picky than could be expected.

One week later:

Mama saw the Misses Bell sitting in Old Mill Square. She says they were "picking" cheerily: How did we get along sans butler and housemaids? How did we eat? Etc.?

Although Beatrice resented being cold-shouldered by the "Art Assassination," she wasn't at all obsessed with attracting attention and winning approval. On the whole, at 39 she had a healthy sense of proportion—a quality almost entirely lacking in Newport in this period—and a certain amount of emotional detachment. At times she seems altogether as amused at the grandees and their laughably outlandish preoccupations as the modern reader.

The historical pageant, a form of entertainment combining the extravagance of a Rose Bowl parade with the solemnity of a funeral procession, was a highlight of almost every social season. Beatrice was reminded of one when she happened to run into "Mrs. Robert Potter of last year's German hate fest." The Potter lineage included a justice of the Supreme Court, a congressman, an ambassador, three Episcopal bishops, a college president and a Union Army general.

Mrs. Potter had charge of the 200th anniversary of Trinity Church pageant last year and impersonated "Germany," who walked about while the other "nations" cut her—until finally she knelt before the church, as exemplified by Dr. Hughes of Trinity. Then the minister lifted fingers of blessing and forgave her! Quite a scandalous performance.

Like the child in the crowd in the tale of "The Emperor's New Clothes," Beatrice refuses to be taken in by the foolishness that passes for sophistication. She was reading Theodore Dreiser and H. G. Wells in this period, biographies of George Washington and Benjamin Franklin, and an anthology of parables told by Abraham Lincoln.

One of the highlights of the Newport season for her was the opening of the Casino Theatre. The discerning eye noticed more than the drama that unfolded on the stage.

Altogether a capable and likeable company and not too tall for the very miniature stage. A woman taking the part of a maid threatened to reach the ceiling. The others fit.

The atmosphere is rather that of an opera in this little playhouse. The play is tolerated without much interest. The curtain lowered, the audience turns to gaze—one at the other.

She was also interested in the dramas enacted outside of the playhouse, and the cast of characters in the swirl of life around her.

Handsome, chauffered cars. Gaily colored cloaks flashing through the darkness. Sailors and their girls walking to the beach. The Italian fruit store all lit up, and the very stout Italian woman sitting complacently, hands folded over her amazing frontal, as she has done these twenty years past. Children come, children marry, grandchildren come and grow up. Still the fat mother with her small, regular features and immense corporation sits on her chair by the sidewalk, viewing the passing show of Bath Road, while her small, blue-eyed husband stands beside her or plies his calling of knife-and-scissor grinder. She is quite a character, the fat Italian mother.

The Italian fruit store couple warmly described in this entry were the grandparents of A. J. Sardella, the Newport man who rescued some of the loveliest of Beatrice's paintings when the Nathan Fleischer collection wound up on a trash pile on Rhode Island Avenue. This footnote to the Beatrice story strangely illuminates one of the central mysteries. Beatrice very definitely had a feeling for the rhythms of life, the passing of time, the change of seasons. If you look at her self-portraits and the double portraits of herself and her mother, you can see that she sometimes painted the same picture over again, more or less, except that she, or she and her mother were a little older. Or they were wearing light wraps instead of fur stoles. These pictures are all life-size; if they were arranged in a gallery in chronological order, the effect would be uncanny. Beatrice, or Beatrice and Adele, would exist on canvas, big as life, at different stages of the life cycle. The poses would be the same, but their clothing would change with the sea-

In a touching twist of irony, Beatrice's "very stout Italian woman" turns out to have been A.J. Sardella's Grandmother.

sons and they would *appear to age* before our eyes. Was this Beatrice's artistic vision? Was she, in this way, attempting to compensate for the fixed and static quality of portraiture? Was she trying to achieve a *living* art, by conveying the illusion of figures moving in time? "Children come, children marry, grandchildren come and grow up." In any event, this sense of rhythm and flow, time and change, is clearly evident in the way she looked at her surroundings, as in these passages written late in September, at the end of the Newport season of 1927, when most of the summer colonists had departed:

> Something unusual and very beautiful in day's calm. The George Bolling Lees—gone. The boardinghouse people—gone. A haunting loveliness in the air. A shadowing of light. The grass a very emerald, fully realized green.

> Painted in the afternoon. Later walked to the library through the green archway of Cliff Avenue, Gibbs Avenue and Old Beach Road. Not a leaf turned on the trees, not a soul walking.

> Very beautiful all morning, growing warmer until at noon it was as lovely as summer.

Beatrice Turner self-portrait (1933) at age 45.

IX

*I*n the summer of 1945, two brave and curious children, nine-year-old Susan King and her eight-and-a-half-year-old cousin Seabury Brady, decided to do something that none of the other kids they played with in Newport ever had the nerve to do. They decided to visit the haunted house on the corner of Cliff and Seaview Avenues. Children naturally considered the rambling old building "haunted," because it was painted black and the person who lived in it was no longer young and kept to herself. Their parents said she was a recluse. If a "recluse" wasn't exactly a "witch," it was anyway close enough to make an imaginative child wonder what she looked like and what she was up to. The neighborhood kids used to throw stones at Cliffside. Haunted houses seem to excite fear, wonder and mischievousness in equal doses. Seabury once shattered one of the ballroom windows. But his curiosity finally got the better of him. He wanted to find out what was inside the house and see who lived there, but was afraid to go alone. So he got Susan to go with him.

In those days, even children understood that if you went to pay somebody a visit, you weren't supposed to go empty-handed. So they went to

Seabury's house on Seaview Avenue and picked a handful of string beans from his mother's victory garden. With this gift-offering in hand, they crossed the street and turned left. Three-quarters of the way up the block, they turned right to enter the grounds, walked a little further past the ivy-covered black veranda, turned left again, climbed the black steps to the black porch and approached the black door of the black house. They felt like Hansel and Gretel. The doorbell was the old-fashioned pull-out kind. When Susan pulled on it, it came off in her hands. Presently, the woman who lived in the house came to the door. Susan thought she was very beautiful and had lovely skin, a peaches-and-cream complexion. She wore a long black skirt and a white blouse; her shoes were badly worn at the heels.

Beatrice Turner thanked the children for the string beans in their outstretched hands, but didn't take them because she said she didn't eat string beans and she didn't cook. But she smiled and graciously invited the children in. She led them on a tour of the ground floor, through one room after another, all filled with paintings—paintings hanging on the walls, and rows and rows of paintings leaning against the walls. The paintings were lifesize portraits, and they towered over a nine-year-old and an eight-and-a-half-year-old. The images were so realistic, it looked as if hundreds of adults were in the house. The tour ended in the ballroom, which was also filled with leaning and hanging paintings. There was one piece of furniture in the ballroom: a grand piano.

Beatrice sat Susan and Seabury down on a window seat, and asked them where they went to school and what they were doing now that school was out, and finally said, "How would you like to come back tomorrow and have your portraits painted? But you must get your parents' permission, so your parents will know where you are."

Susan was something of a tomboy and had been dressed like Seabury in t-shirt and shorts. She also wore a sailor hat with the brim turned down, like a cloche. But as long as she was going to have her portrait painted, she thought she ought to dress up. When the cousins returned the next day, Seabury had on the same t-shirt and shorts, but Susan wore her best dress.

Beatrice had apparently wanted to paint her as a little tomboy. "Where's your sailor hat?" Beatrice asked. "You must go right home and change back to what you wore yesterday."

"But I don't live down the street," Susan said. "I live a couple of miles away, in Middletown, and I walked here."

"Oh, that's all right, then we'll just paint you this way," Beatrice said, and for the next six weeks, the children returned every day to sit for their portrait. They brought Beatrice candy bars every day, because Beatrice hinted that she liked candy. She posed the children separately and never kept them sitting for too long. While one sat for her, the other was free to explore Cliffside. The doors of the upstairs rooms were all closed; Seabury loved to run upstairs and fling them open. It was difficult to get him to sit still and pose for any length of time.

Between sittings, there was plenty of time for fun. Beatrice entertained the children by singing to them and accompanying herself on the piano. She sang "The Battle Hymn of the Republic." The piano in the ballroom was terribly out of tune, but no one seemed to mind. Beatrice treated the kids like company. She knew how to talk to them without talking down to them, how to enter their world. There was a hole in the ballroom window about the size of a dime, and one day, when they all sat down on the long window seat, they sat so close to the hole, you could hardly avoid seeing it. Seabury stared guiltily at the floor, trying not to notice the hole and the small, streamlined pattern of shatter that surrounded it. But a moment later he was able to relax because Beatrice let him off the hook. She made light of the damage, explaining it away as the imprint of a fairy's slipper and concocted a story about fairies and windows.

When the portrait was finished, it showed Susan and Seabury sitting side by side. Susan has a book of fairy tales in her lap, and Seabury holds a toy PT boat. They're not playing, giggling or fidgeting in the picture, but are quietly looking beyond the frame of the composition. They're looking at the world—not the world familiar to adults, but the world that children see. The world we all saw when we were eight-and-a-half or nine years old: a world of infinite wonder where all things were possible, all roads lay ahead and on all journeys only the first precious steps had yet been taken. Beatrice had painted Susan and Seabury's portrait, and had also painted a portrait of childhood.

The children were asked to bring their mothers around to look at the picture. On that day, Susan and Seabury heard Beatrice mention the price of the painting, and each hoped their mother would buy it so they could take the

*Susan King and Seabury Brady were surprise models
for Beatrice in 1945.*

portrait home. But neither Mrs. King nor Mrs. Brady liked the picture. Seabury's mother thought the painted Seabury didn't look at all like himself. Of course, the real Seabury never sat still long enough for Beatrice to get a precise fix on him. On the other hand, the painted Susan was a spitting image, but her mother thought Beatrice had made Susan look too old. So when Susan and Seabury walked out of Cliffside for the last time, the painting remained behind, hanging on Beatrice Turner's wall.

Years later, when the war was over, the children's fathers were home and Beatrice Turner had died, Seabury's father received a call from a friend of his who was in real estate. The real estate man had been inside Cliffside, had seen the painting of the two children and had recognized Seabury. Seabury's father knew that Susan and Seabury had posed for Beatrice during the last summer of the war. The family had told him that Susan's likeness was truer-to-life. Since the entire Turner estate was now one big liquidation sale, Seabury's father bought the painting and gave it to his niece.

Seabury Brady married, had a family of his own and died of heart and lung disease in 1989. Susan King still lives in Middletown, Rhode Island, the next town over from Newport. Before he died, Seabury told Susan that he would like to give the painting to his children, if she didn't want it any longer. The painting had been in her attic for decades. On the day of Seabury's funeral, Susan took the painting down from the attic and had it framed. But for some reason she couldn't part with it. She hung it on her wall instead, an ever-present reminder of a wonderful childhood memory.

"She was so sweet to us. She was such a delightful person," Ms. King said recently, reminiscing about Beatrice. "I was about 12 when she died. I remember reading the *LIFE* magazine article and being upset that they made her seem so odd." A number of other people who have contacted Win Baker during the search for the paintings also have personal memories of Beatrice Turner. These are fifty-year-old memories, and they're often fuzzy and incomplete. But they add up; they form a composite. The Beatrice we meet in this way, through the eyes of people who came in contact with her, one way or another, is the Beatrice of the diaries—the engaging, discerning Beatrice who was to some extent involved with the world—not the Beatrice of the sensationalist press, the "tragic, narcissist recluse" as Win Baker puts it. Joan Shand, who was a student nurse at University Hospital in Philadelphia, where Beatrice died of cancer, uses almost the same words to describe Beatrice as Susan King: "She was a delightful woman. Charming. Never complained, even though she must have obviously been in a certain amount of discomfort." Beatrice asked Shand to pose for her when she was off-duty and painted two portraits of her. Shand remembers that Beatrice had a girlfriend who regularly visited her at the hospital and brought her paints and brushes. So much for *LIFE*'s assertion that Beatrice led a "secluded life" and "saw nobody."

Philadelphia student nurse Joan Shand was rewarded for her kindness in caring for Beatrice at University Hospital in 1948. These are the last works of art Beatrice Turner is known to have completed.

Directly across Seaview Avenue from Cliffside is a large, three-story white shingle house with almost as many peaks as windows. The building has recently been converted to condominium apartments, but was previously the Bella Vista Guest Manor, a stopping place favored by Gypsy Rose Lee, Charlton Heston and other theatre people who played the Newport Casino, and musicians like pianist Hazel Scott who performed at the Newport Jazz and Folk Festivals. The proprietor of the Guest Manor, the late Mrs. Rosamond Hendel, came to Newport during World War II to direct U.S.O. activities in Rhode Island and southern Massachusetts. Due to the wartime housing crunch, she wound up renting an apartment from Nathan Fleischer. Fleischer first converted Cliff Lawn to an apartment house before he turned the mansion into a hotel. Bella Vista was also an apartment house at this time, but these apartments were exclusively for servicemen and women and their families. Mrs. Hendel moved into Bella Vista in 1943 and opened the Guest Manor after the war. She became great friends with Nat Fleischer and helped him stage the Beatrice Turner exhibit at Cliff Lawn. For five summers, from the time she moved into Bella Vista until Beatrice Turner's death, she was Beatrice Turner's next-door neighbor.

Mrs. Hendel, interviewed in 1993, remembered Beatrice as "a very private and lonesome person. She was friendly with my family and me, but she wasn't out very much to be seen. She mowed her own lawn in the mornings with a push mower. She wore long, elegant gloves and covered the wooden handles of the lawnmower with newspaper so she wouldn't get her gloves dirty. That's when we exchanged our 'Good mornings' and 'How are yous.' But that's as far as she'd let anyone approach her."

Rosamond Hendel's daughter, Paula Smith, now 65, was just entering her teens at this time and used to

Rosamond Hendel and daughter Paula Smith were Beatrice's next door neighbors.

pass Cliffside every day on her way to and from school. She was a homely kid, sensitive and impressionable, and always ran past the black house because it frightened and depressed her. "On rainy, dreary days," she recalls, "the imagination went haywire." Getting off the bus on her way home from school one day, she suddenly came face to face with the very genteel Beatrice Turner. She had only seen Beatrice from afar before, when Beatrice was mowing her lawn, and was stunned to receive a cheerful greeting.

"Hello, Paula. How are you? Isn't it a lovely day?"

After that, Paula Smith wasn't afraid of Cliffside anymore.

Mrs. Hendel said that Beatrice had one close friend, a Newport woman named Marjorie Wilson who also lived alone and was an artist. Ms. Wilson died in the 1960s. Someone else who got to know Beatrice during this period was a petite, attractive and radiant young woman of 17. Mary Atwood Sharp was an army brat; her father was a colonel, and the family moved around from post to post. The only place she really considered "home" was her grandmother's house in Newport, where Mary spent her summer vacations. Her family worshipped at Trinity Church and knew Beatrice Turner as a member of the congregation. Beatrice walked to church; Mrs. Sharp's family drove and often gave Beatrice a lift home. On one of these occasions, Beatrice asked Mary to pose for her. Beatrice seems to have been as interested in painting other people's portraits as she was in painting her own. She also asked a couple of Mary's girlfriends to pose for her. The ballroom at Cliffside was Beatrice's studio. Mrs. Sharp remembers it as an enormous space, two stories high, full of paintings—many lifesize—from floor to ceiling. In addition to the self-portraits, there were paintings of Beatrice's parents and numerous paintings of her acquaintances.

Beatrice first posed Mary in a white dress in front of blue hydrangeas and painted a portrait the artist called "Summer and Seventeen." She had her blue-eyed, blonde-haired subject sit for a couple of other portraits throughout the early 1940s, and when Mary Atwood married Lieutenant Commander Roger Rittenhouse Sharp of the U.S. Navy in 1945, just after her twentieth birthday, Beatrice painted her in her wedding dress. This was a nearly lifesize composition. "Beatrice romanticized everything," Mrs. Sharp said. "She had angels perched on great colonnades behind me, and the chamomiles flowed over my white satin gown like there was no tomorrow."

Mary Atwood Sharp at 17, 18, 19 and 20 wasn't forward enough or curious enough to ask Beatrice Turner why she dressed the way she did or painted herself so many times. They made small talk, but didn't have any intimate conversations. Like Susan King and Joan Shand, she simply remembers Beatrice as a gracious and considerate woman. Mrs. Sharp once took Beatrice to lunch on fashionable Bellevue Avenue, where they dined at La Forge Tea Room (now La Forge Casino Restaurant) overlooking the championship tennis courts at the Newport Casino. "As we walked up the Avenue," Mrs. Sharp said, "she asked me if I felt embarrassed to be seen with her. She wore old-fashioned tight-bodiced, scoop-necked dresses and her skirt almost down to the ankle. She must've used corn starch to powder her face; it was quite white. But her health wasn't too marvelous either. And when she went out she always wore a great big hat, one of those black things that was kind of stiff. She was different and unusual, but in every way sweet and kind as far as I was concerned. I said, 'No, I didn't.'"

Beatrice was proud of her portrait of Mary in her wedding dress and decided to have a tea to show it off. She drafted Mary to help her entertain. On

*Beatrice Turner painted Mary Atwood Sharp
in her wedding dress in 1945.*

a Sunday afternoon during the summer of 1945, some seven or eight people
whom Beatrice knew from Philadelphia or from Trinity Church and the Art
Association of Newport, including some Bellevue Avenue types, sat on chairs
Beatrice and Mary had dragged into the ballroom, ate cookies, drank tea and
looked at the paintings. The principal guest was a Lord Fermoy, the son of an

English baron and an American heiress. So much for the statement in the Hearst publication, the *American Weekly*, that for Beatrice Turner "There was no world outside her mirror and her mind's-eye."

LIFE and the *American Weekly* printed almost verbatim the story Nathan Fleischer sold them. Staff writers condensed the story for *LIFE* and embellished it for the Hearst Sunday supplement, but in neither case was any additional reporting done. This was unfortunate because Fleischer had already edited the story before he presented it to the media. He selected the parts of the story that were saleable, and he started seeing the story as saleable and shaping it that way the moment he first encountered it.

Win Baker has astutely observed that Fleischer could not have picked out sixty-plus Turner paintings *at random* and wound up with the collection he exhibited at Cliff Lawn. In fact, the rescue of the Turner paintings wasn't quite as heroic and romantic an act in reality as it was in legend. Fleischer did not swoop down on the city dump like Errol Flynn and yank art work off the bonfire. Rosamond Hendel said he bought the paintings from the auctioneer who disposed of the Turner estate. Cliffside was open during the estate sale to people who wanted to examine the contents of the house and bid on them. The man who recognized Seabury Brady in the painting of Susan and Seabury had some sort of business in the house at this time. Mary Atwood Sharp's mother came to inquire about the portraits of her daughter and subsequently bought them. Mrs. Hendel entered the house just out of curiosity. Apparently, so did Nat Fleischer.

Like everyone else who entered the house, Fleischer saw a lot of paintings. He saw the portraits of Beatrice's acquaintances that Mary Atwood Sharp remembers seeing. He also saw numerous landscapes and seascapes. Beatrice painted her surroundings *repeatedly*. Her will, written in 1940 just after her mother died, cites among numerous bequests "studies in watercolor and pastel, framed and unframed, of gardens, cliffs and ocean at Newport, Rhode Island." She bequeathed these works to the Historical Society of Newport "to be preserved as records of the visual beauty of Newport from 1907 to 1940." The Historical Society did not honor that bequest. Only one Turner landscape survives today—a handsome, shimmering study of the Cliffs and the sea, with the sun just breaking through the clouds. Win Baker found it on the back(!) of a still life he bought from a Philadelphia woman, Mrs. C. B. Baukus, who had bought it years earlier in a Miami art gallery. The work is now part of the Cliffside Inn collection and is exhibited in a room named in honor of it, the Seascape Room.

All of the Newport studies that existed in 1940 and any additional landscapes or seascapes Beatrice might have completed after the will was written presumably were in Cliffside when Nathan Fleischer walked through the house in 1948. These too he mentally set aside. He saw the self-portraits, and while he was looking at the myriad lovely, haunting images, he was also seeing himself exhibiting them and telling a story about them, the "story of egosexia." The uniqueness of Nathan Fleischer was that whatever he saw himself doing (running for mayor, opening a hotel, becoming a hypnotist), he did. He selected a range of pictures showing Beatrice as she aged from her late teens to her late fifties, and found diary entries and other material that supported the story he wanted to tell.

That story, if slanted, was at least consistent with the folklore that existed in Newport at the time and continues to exist today. People talked about Beatrice all her adult life. Even now, oldtimers who either were children in the 1940s, like Susan King, or young adults, like Mary Atwood Sharp, and who remember the lady in the big hats and long skirts, will tell you tales their parents told them about Beatrice. They believed those stories when they heard them in their youth, and they believe them still. Nat Fleischer heard the same stories and wove them into his narrative, like the tale that Beatrice refused to let her father be buried until she finished painting his portrait in death. That story passed directly from Fleischer to *LIFE* magazine.

According to the more baroque variations on the theme, Andrew Turner never left Cliffside, but was buried in the basement like the victims in *Arsenic and Old Lace*. Or, what was left of him by 1948 was found upstairs, like Norman Bates' mother. In all fairness to Fleischer, the truth was not to be found in Newport, even if he were inclined to look for it. The truth was in a newspaper archive in Philadelphia.

Beatrice Turner self–portrait sketch (1936) at age 48.

X

On October 4, 1913, Andrew Turner made the front page of the *Philadelphia Inquirer*. This was 13 days after he died and two days before he was buried. The headline adroitly emphasized two of the three perennial themes of mass circulation publications: death and money.[*]

Dreaded Burial Alive; Keep Body For Two Weeks
Andrew J. Turner Died Sep 21; Funeral Oct 6
Recurrence of Dream of Brother Reviving in Grave
Haunted Cotton Broker

"Haunted during life by fear of being buried alive," the story began, "Andrew J. Turner, a cotton broker who lived at 2322 Spruce Street, often begged his wife not to permit his body to be interred after his apparent death until

---

[*] Sex didn't enter the Turner saga until Nathan Fleischer found Beatrice's nude studies.

she was satisfied that there was no possibility of life remaining in it." Andrew apparently believed that his brother, who predeceased him, *had* been buried alive. He had a recurring dream "in which he saw his brother, who died many years ago, seeking to escape from a casket in which he had been interred. He talked of this dream on many occasions and said he feared a like fate."

Andrew Turner was 49 and had been suffering from kidney disease for about three years. Late in September of 1913, he and his father-in-law, Edwin Jackson Haas, then a member of the Turner household, had returned from Newport to open the Spruce Street townhouse, which had been locked for the summer. Turner and Haas arrived in Philadelphia on the night of September 21, a Saturday. Haas went to bed. Turner, unbeknownst to the *Inquirer*, sat down and wrote a letter to his wife and daughter, who remained at Cliffside. In that letter, he composed the poem beginning, "I dreamed that I dwelt in a house of black/Located in the land of Arcadia . . ." He was found dead the next morning.

Adele and Beatrice were immediately summoned home from Newport. "On their arrival," the *Inquirer* reported, "Mrs. Turner took charge of the body and refused to permit plans to be made for a funeral in the near future. She said that she was determined to have the body of her husband kept in the house until absolutely unmistakable signs of death appeared, feeling that by so doing she would be carrying out the wishes of Mr. Turner." Adele at first held out hope that her husband's premonition had been correct and that he had erroneously been pronounced dead. The reality of the situation, however, could not be denied. She shortly accepted the fact that he would not be restored to her and allowed the body to be embalmed. "But she said that she felt that she should carry out the wishes of her husband despite this fact," and would not permit the embalmed remains to be removed from the house and buried.

The undertakers were apparently in and out of 2322 Spruce Street on a daily basis during these two weeks, and their comings and goings did not go unnoticed. "Crepe on the door and the frequent visits of the undertaker," said the *Inquirer*, "have so aroused the neighbors that notification was sent yesterday to the Department of Health." The *Inquirer* could assume that its readers had a general sense of who the neighbors were. Spruce Street was a highly fashionable address in Philadelphia in 1913, a classic tintype of turn-of-the-century gentility: cobblestones, cast-iron lampposts, shade trees, a row of brownstones. The leading figures in the political, social, economic and cultural life of the city occupied those row houses. They included prominent members of the "first families" of Philadelphia—the Morrises, Cadwaladers, Coxes, Meades, Coateses, Wetherills, Lippincotts, Clarks, Woods, Lennigs, Dallases—all of whom lived on Spruce from roughly the 1300 block to the 2400 block. George Dallas Dixon of the Pennsylvania Railroad, the dean of American railroad traffic officers, resided at 2004 Spruce; his grandfather, George Mifflin Dallas, had served as Vice President of the United States under James K. Polk. Colonel Josiah Granville Leach of 2118 Spruce was the originator of Flag Day, which is still observed on June 14 in honor of the adoption in 1777 of the stars and stripes. His daughter, May Atherton Leach, was a founding member of the Genealogical Society of Pennsylvania. Aging Horace Pettit at 2400 Spruce was one of the foremost corporate lawyers in Philadelphia and an authority on patent law. Porter Farquharson Cope at 2418 was editor and publisher of several Philadelphia weeklies and secretary of something called the Anti-Vaccination League of America.

The Turners' immediate neighbors were a banker, Jesse Williams, and a judge, Maxwell Stevenson. As might be expected, given the status of the complainants, the Department of Health promptly dispatched an inspector to 2322 Spruce. But, explained the *Inquirer*, "there was nothing in the law which would prevent a body being kept in the house for that length of time provided there was nothing on which to base a complaint of a nuisance." Nevertheless, the pressure on Adele Turner to relinquish the remains must have been enormous. But she would not weaken. "The widow takes the ground that so long as the presence of her husband's body in the house does not constitute a menace to the neighborhood she is privileged to keep it there," the *Inquirer* said. "The undertakers have made daily visits to the house and have done all that they could to preserve the body. The corpse rests on a death couch in the front room of the house."

Mrs. Turner's decision to fulfill her husband's wishes, despite the opposition of a powerful community—a rather gallant gesture, when the facts are clear—was undoubtedly the source of the stigma that would attach to the Turner women, mother and daughter, for the rest of their lives. The postmortem scene was followed by another shocking and macabre act: the painting of Cliffside black. Many of the Spruce Street elite (the John Cadwaladers of 2100 Spruce and the Bertram Lippincotts of 1712, for example) were also members of the Newport summer colony. News traveled back and forth from Newport to Philadelphia, and the Turners' reputation never recovered. By the time Nathan Fleischer wandered through Cliffside 35 years later, the pivotal role Adele played in the drama was forgotten and Beatrice was falsely cast as the person who kept the body of Andrew Turner at home for two weeks.

The folklore was correct in one respect: during those two weeks, Beatrice did paint a portrait of her father in death. In fact, Fleischer found the death portrait at Cliffside and purchased it for his collection. But when twenty-five-year-old Beatrice moved her easel and palette into the front room of the Spruce Street house, where the corpse of Andrew Turner rested on a "death couch," she wasn't, as Fleischer and a sensationalist press assumed, acting on a morbid and ghastly impulse that flew into her head without any context whatsoever. Posthumous mourning portraiture was an American tradition.

Beatrice's father and mother were born, respectively, in 1864 and 1865, and were married in 1886. The other member of the household in 1913, her grandfather, was born in 1836. They weren't twentieth-century people, they were nineteenth-century people, and nineteenth-century people had a different attitude toward death and bereavement than people do today. Nineteenth-century people weren't expected to put their grief behind them and "get on with their lives" as quickly as possible. They were expected to honor the deceased by displaying their grief publicly and elaborately. Posthumous mourning portraiture flourished in this context.

Phoebe Lloyd, an art historian at the University of Pennsylvania, contributed a meticulously researched, well-written and definitive essay on mourning portaiture to *A Time to Mourn: Expressions of Grief in Nineteenth Century America*, a companion volume for an exhibition of the same name that opened on May 24, 1980, at the Museums at Stony Brook, on Long Island, New York. Lloyd found that the practice of commissioning these paintings was so widespread that ads extolling an artist's skill in "taking portraits" of "deceased persons" were run in the newspapers of the day. "Indeed," she wrote, "so necessary might posthumous mourning portrait commissions be to an artist's livelihood, that it was the fortunate artist who could disdain such work." Even Thomas Cole, the great landscape painter and founder of the Hudson River School, was forced to accept at least one such commission.

Beatrice's posthumous mourning portrait of Andrew J. Turner:
"Daddy in Death" (1913).

The posthumous images were commissioned during the mourning period to provide a continuing presence for the deceased in the life of the family. The artist worked carefully and diligently to bring the deceased "to life." Lloyd was able to document the process in one instance:

> An early example of the posthumous mourning portrait is Ralph E. W. Earle's rendering of Sarah Louisa Spence. The daughter of a prominent Nashville family, she had succumbed overnight to cholera, and her disconsolate parents promptly ordered her portrait. Every effort was made by the artist to achieve an exact likeness. He took measurements from the corpse and worked with a lock of her hair for color. Sarah's parents also supplied Earle with a double portrait of her and her mother, painted when the child was five. Her half-sister was called in to pose because she had the same hazel eyes. The large commissioned canvas, 48 by 66 inches, assured that nine-year-old Sarah would appear life-size.

The tradition of posthumous mourning portraiture followed certain conventions. The paintings were generally life-size, and the deceased was represented as if alive. A symbol was used to indicate death. Lloyd continues:

> Costumed in the clothes she wore in life, Sarah Louisa Spence greets the viewer as though she were about to step down from her proscenium stage space into the viewer's own. Only the rose she holds betokens her altered condition. Viewers of the period would have known that roses held downward or drooping from a broken stem symbolized an innocent life cut short. In Earle's portrait, Sarah Louisa Spence is intended to exist in a twilight state between the quick and the dead.

Beatrice Turner must have seen numerous examples of posthumous mourning portraiture. She was not only familiar with the genre and its conventions but effectively mastered the format in her portrait of "Daddy in Death." The portrait is missing and presumed lost, but was photographed in black-and-white by John Hopf, and the photograph survives. It is difficult to tell from the photograph if the image is life-size, but it is certainly lifelike. Andrew is sitting erect in a large, upholstered chair, and there is a cushion behind him. Whether, as *LIFE* alleged, Beatrice "propped up his embalmed body in a chair with pillows," or just visualized him sitting erect, is unknown. He is handsomely dressed in jacket, vest, collar and tie, and holds a closed book in his hands—the symbol Beatrice chose to signify death.

Andrew had large eyes, which his daughter inherited. In the portrait, his eyes are open, and he's looking directly at the viewer. There is a remarkable innocence and clarity in his gaze. The veils have been removed; human frailties have vanished. He perceives a deeper truth. He is aware of his own destiny. Branches of trees seem to be flooded with light in the background. He is sitting in an upholstered chair, but the chair is not in its accustomed setting. It is not indoors. The juxtaposition of armchair and outdoors creates an extraordinary sense of displacement from the ordinary. It is a powerful image.

Nathan Fleischer exhibited a diary page on which Beatrice, at 25, presumably, wrote what she was thinking when she painted the death portrait. Her reflections apparently filled more than one page; the words at the top begin in the middle of a thought. Fleischer highlighted three sentences at the bottom of the page: "My drawing of Papa in death is the only face approaching god-hood I have drawn. Can it be I do not strike the right fire? At all events nature now holds me in its spell." The curiosity seekers who filed through the exhibit at Cliff Lawn looked at the self-portraits and the death portrait and the "god-hood" quote, heard the disembodied voice from behind the black drapes, and had the same creepy, melodramatic sort of entertainment experience they enjoyed when they went home, turned the radio on and listened to *The Shadow*. It was a great show, but Beatrice didn't think that her father was a god, a saint or a prophet any more than she was a "victim of ego-sexia."

On the same diary page, Beatrice described the human body as "the golden earthly setting of a gem of never-dying fire." She believed that the purpose of life was the polishing of that gem, and that her goal as an artist was to portray the "earthly garb" in such a way as to reveal the inner, spiritual dimension. She felt she came closest to that goal in her portrait of "Daddy in Death." This was the meaning of mourning portraiture.

"The posthumous mourning portrait functioned as an icon for the bereaved," said Phoebe Lloyd. "Contemplating it was part of the mourning rit-ual." Sarah Louisa Spence in the Earle portrait was "intended to exist in a twi-light state between the quick and the dead." Discussing another example of the genre, Lloyd said, "Through the medium of a painted portrait," the subject "returns from where the living have not yet been." Elsewhere in her essay, she refers to mourning portraiture as "attempted communion between the living and the dead." Like all expressions of spirituality, whether in oral traditions or scripture, ceremony or art, the posthumous mourning portrait expressed a symbolic connection between what ordinary human beings can perceive and what we can't. Beatrice understood mourning portraiture in its symbolic sense. And because she did, her portrait of "Daddy in Death" is the key to unlocking one of the perennial mysteries of her life.

When Nat Fleischer found the posthumous mourning portrait of An-drew Turner at Cliffside, he knew he had identified an important artifact in the Beatrice story. But he made the wrong connection. He naturally assumed that the folklore was correct—that Andrew died at Cliffside and that Beatrice kept the body in the house until the painting was finished. But Andrew died in Philadelphia, and the portrait was painted there, in the front room of 2322 Spruce Street. What was it doing in Newport? Why did Beatrice and her mother carry it with them on the 24-hour taxi, train and boat trip from Penn-sylvania? Why wasn't that painting in the house where Andrew and Adele had lived together for a quarter of a century, the house they had occupied since a year and a half after they got married, and where their only child was born?

The answer is entirely consistent with the symbolic understanding of posthumous mourning portraiture. Since the painting represented the conti-nuity of Andrew Turner, the "gem of never-dying fire" that was—and is—An-drew Turner, by enshrining that portrait at Cliffside, having the house painted black and never having it repainted, Beatrice and Adele were able to fulfill Andrew's last earthly dream and sentiment.

They made it possible for him to "dwell," among his loved ones, in a house of black located in the land of Arcadia.

It was a truly magnificent gesture.

Beatrice Turner's "House of Black" painting.

Beatrice Turner self-portrait (1945) at age 57.

XI

"**S**ometimes I get very angry at Nathan Fleischer for the way he exploited her," Win Baker said, in a recent conversation during afternoon tea in the parlor of the Cliffside Inn. "Then I have to stop and think if he hadn't done what he did, we wouldn't be sitting here talking today. Because, however those paintings were saved and however many he had, and however many diary pages he had and how he got them, and whether he went to the fire, and the exact details—who knows? We only know what other people say and what we think is true, and what he told other people, which may or may not be true. The fact is, one way or the other, he kept the story of Beatrice Turner alive, because if it hadn't been for him, there would be no story, there would be no tape, there would be no article in *LIFE* magazine. So, on the one hand, you can condemn him for portraying her in an exploitative way; on the other hand, you can also say, thank goodness he did."

Win paused for a moment, glancing over at the 1921 double portrait of Beatrice and her mother, the only Turner portrait that never left Cliffside, the painting he saw when he first visited the inn in 1989. Adele, shown in profile, faces the viewer's left. Beatrice is glancing off past the viewer's right shoulder. The wistful, searching look of the thirty-three-year-old beauty in Victorian clothes still beguiles. "What we do know is she painted a hell of a lot of pictures of herself, and that's pretty unusual," he said. "She's far more sober and serious, and much less crazy than we originally thought. Though, the more I consider that, the harder it is to understand the idiosyncracies."

Nat Fleischer would undoubtedly be amused. No matter how bright and witty the diaries are, how many people you talk to who had contact with her and how many paintings come to light that aren't self-portraits, the questions he first posed as far back as the Truman administration inevitably recur: "Can you imagine a woman who spent her entire lifetime looking in a mirror and creating thousands—yes, thousands—of oil paintings of herself? Can you picture a woman who right up until 1948 wore the clothes of the Victorian era . . ."

Living as we do in an information age, we generally suppose that "understanding the idiosyncracies" would require more information about Beatrice than is currently available. But there is an old Central Asian story that, among other things, puts information and understanding in a different light. This is the story of the villager who rode across the border of his country every week on a donkey. The border guards suspected that the villager was smuggling something over the frontier, but they never found anything of value on his person and had no further information to go on. Years and years later, the villager and one of the border guards, both retired now, met at a cafe in another land. "So what were you smuggling out of our country?" the former guard asked. The old rogue answered, "Donkeys."

The available information may be more than adequate if you look at it the right way. What happens if you put aside all the usual things that have been said about Beatrice and look past appearances? What happens if you look at things from different angles? Instead of asking why something is the way it is, what happens if you were to ask why it wasn't otherwise, like the location of the posthumous mourning portrait of Andrew Turner? What happens, say, if you were to look at the 1921 double portrait and imagine that, instead of a picture hat, Beatrice was wearing a cloche hat, and instead of the frills and lace and the ankle-length skirt, she had on a sleek, long-waisted ensemble that came to below the knee? What would people say about *this* picture? If the other parts of the Beatrice story were the same, but she wore clothes that were fashionable in 1921, what would people's reaction be?

People would say about Beatrice what Beatrice said about Isadora Duncan and Julia Hoyt. They would say she was ahead of her time. She didn't just sit back on a lawn chair, polishing her nails and waiting for "the right man" to come along. She could have: she was a woman of some means. No, they would say, she took an active interest in the world around her and pursued a vocation. Never mind that she didn't support herself as an artist; wealthy men and women often devote themselves to administrative, intellectual or artistic pursuits from which they derive little if any income. Look at her behavior. She went out and bought paints, brushes, canvasses, pencils, sketch pads. She mixed the paints. She worked in oil and watercolor. She sketched, she touched up and added finishing touches. Every single day, she worked hard refining her skills, developing her craft.

The "smuggled donkey" in the Beatrice story, the element we lose sight of because she did wear old-fashioned clothes, was that *she wasn't an old-fashioned woman*. She was modern in the important sense that early on she dedicated herself to a career, a profession, and worked at it every day of her adult life. But she was a modern woman in a Victorian disguise. Why? Because she had to be.

Suppose at age 21 she had said to her parents, "I want to pursue a career." Her parents would have hit the roof. Andrew and Adele Turner were old-fashioned, nineteenth-century people. By satisfying them, by living at home, quitting art school, accompanying them to Newport every year—being, outwardly, the proper Victorian young lady they wanted her to be—she was able to pursue a career without incurring their displeasure. Adele Turner painted; she also played the piano. Gentlewomen were supposed to cultivate these and other talents. They were supposed to know how to dance; they were supposed to know how to entertain. But they were supposed to be dilettantes, not professionals. Beatrice led "a life she did not choose," because she wasn't free to live the life she wanted.

But she wanted her freedom very badly.

In the 1921 dual portrait, Beatrice is standing so close to her mother that it almost looks as if Mama is leading her by the hand. Adele's hands are actually clasped in front of her, but you have to look twice to notice that. Imagine, however, that this tableau captured a scene that occurred at a real moment in time.

The Turners, say, had entered the lobby of the Casino Theatre. People are milling around. Something catches Beatrice's eye; she looks off to the side. What would happen the very next instant? The lobby doors would open, people would start forward and Mama would say, "Come, Beatrice, don't dawdle."

The 1921 painting is a moment of freedom, as are almost all the other extant dual portraits of Beatrice and Adele. Mama's back is almost always half-turned in these compositions, and in the portraits Beatrice painted of her mother individually. Adele is engrossed in her own thoughts and unaware of what's going on around her, because when her back was turned, or she was preoccupied or not noticing, Beatrice could think, do, see, or be anything she wanted. She relished those moments of freedom and relived them on canvas.

On June 28, 1927, Beatrice wrote in her diary:

> Started to paint on an old canvas a study of the huge, deep blue and pale pink Canterbury bells in the center of the driveway. Mama objected to my working in the sun. She was right, but I think I could have done it sans ill effects, however.

Beatrice was 39 years old—and her mother still couldn't leave her alone. She wanted to be left alone, she wanted to be free. But she was also afraid of freedom. All of her life, her parents communicated a very strong and consistent message to her, the same message her mother reiterated on June 28, 1927. They told her that the world is a bad place. Don't look at nude models in an artists' life class. Don't be seen with a boy on the Cliff Walk. Don't stay out in the sun. That's the message she had heard since the cradle: *Don't*. Don't go out there, people will talk, bad things will happen to you.

In 1907, shortly after the Turners bought Swann Villa, an item about Andrew Turner appeared in "Town Topics," the gossip column of the old *Newport Herald*:

> The other day Mr. Turner was noted at a Thames Street fish emporium where after purchasing two crabs he gave such detailed instructions as to where to send them that the thought occurred that were Mr. Turner to someday go to the expense of buying a bluefish he would probably have it accompanied to the Cliffs by a brass band.

This is not a direct quote from "Town Topics." The quotation is from "Daily Doings." Beatrice reproduced the item verbatim in her diary when she reported what "Town Topics" babbled about her and her mother twenty years later. ("The Turners, mother and daughter of Philadelphia, strolling on Bellevue Avenue in costumes similar to those they have worn for years presumably in the belief that one good turner deserves another.") Andrew gave precise, detailed, meticulous instructions for having the crabs delivered because, in his view, if he didn't give precise instructions, the crabs either wouldn't get delivered or would spoil along the way—bad things would happen. Such was life with Father. He didn't even think he could be buried without error. He was as strict and severe with his daughter as he was with the fishmonger. All her life, Beatrice was told to do exactly *this* and not *that*, sit here, don't lean, don't slouch, don't slurp—because bad things would happen to her out in the world if she didn't rigorously adhere to instructions.

The bulk of our learning is completed at an amazingly early age. We absorb familial, social and cultural messages, the messages form into a pattern and the pattern hardens into conditioned responses. Beatrice clearly got the message. She really did paint herself living a life that only existed in her imagination. On canvas, she is her own woman, free of anyone's influence or any sort of conditioning. She usually portrayed herself as a strong, effective, competent woman. In many situations of daily life, as in the encounter with Officer Casey, she could be strong, effective and competent. But that wasn't what she was really like.

She admired actress Julia Hoyt and empathized with her when Hoyt was largely snubbed by the audience at the Casino theatre:

> I do not know if the play shocked their moral sense, as it well might, or if they disapproved of the revealing dress, or resented her quite real beauty, or were simply "not amused," a la Queen Victoria.

"She waited in the dressing room at the close of the performance for congratulations and congratulators who did not appear," Beatrice wrote. "Mr. Shafter Howard was with her, and Dr. Luce ran through the crowd crosswise to meet her."

I should have liked to, *but* . . .

The strong, effective, competent woman we meet in many of the self-portraits would have marched right up to Julia Hoyt regardless of what anyone might have thought. The real Beatrice was not that woman. The real Beatrice was a vulnerable, inhibited woman who had been taught in no uncertain terms that the world is a bad place where bad things will happen. The real Beatrice was the kind of woman played to perfection by Joan Fontaine in the classic movies *Rebecca* and *Jane Eyre*, a victim of a severe and restrictive upbringing who has not yet had the kinds of experiences that in the course of the film bring out her strength, effectiveness and competence. The real Beatrice was the woman portrayed in the flaming self-portrait, that astonishing image of a young woman drawn to the threshold of darkness and light, and what she is simultaneously attracted to and intimidated by is the prospect of *her own freedom*.

It may not be a coincidence that the flaming self-portrait was painted in 1923, during a period when American women were crossing a cultural threshold. The post-World War I era was a period of sexual revolution, a transition between the Victorian morality of the nineteenth century and the "anything goes" spirit, as Cole Porter put it, of the twentieth. Given the extremes of restriction in the pre-war era, the sexual revolution of the 1920s may have been even more profound than that of the 1960s. The changes were enormous. As the stock market rose through the 1920s, so too did women's hemlines, climbing from six or seven inches off the ground all the way to the knee. The layers of clothing with which women encumbered themselves meanwhile lessened considerably. It took an estimated 19 1/4 yards of material to equip a woman for an outing in the pre-war era—by the late 1920s, a mere seven yards would suffice. Victorian conventions were cast off along with the corsets and petticoats. Women bobbed their hair. They freely applied vampish lipstick and rouge. They smoked, drank and swore in public, and brazenly rejected the double standard of sexual conduct.

Popular authors included thinkers like Sigmund Freud, Carl Jung and Havelock Ellis, who were not officially in the business of supplanting traditional morality and promoting sexual candor, and writers like Maxwell Bodenheim, who were. Rich young women of the 1920s, like Emily Davies, the future Mrs. William H. Vanderbilt, whose suicide Beatrice noted in her diary,

Beatrice Turner's notable "flaming" self-portrait (1923), so-called because of the fire-like orange and red hues reflected in Beatrice's enigmatic gaze.

read Bodenheim's best-selling Jazz Age novels *Replenishing Jessica* and *Naked on Roller Skates*, decamped from the family estate and descended on New York. A couple of young heiresses would share an apartment on Park Avenue and open a little boutique. In the evenings, they would flock to the neighborhood speakeasies to violate the Volstead Act and kick up their heels to full throttle renditions of "Bye Bye Blackbird," "Hello, Bluebird" and "Breezin' Along With the Breeze." As to what would happen next, the historian Samuel Eliot Morison in *The Oxford History of the American People* quotes an "ironical Irish journalist" who, in 1921, "after seeing for himself American post-war mores remarked, 'Unbalanced by prolonged contemplation of the tedious virtues of New England, a generation has arisen whose great illusion is that the transvaluation of all values may be effected by promiscuity.'"

Adele Tull Haas Turner would not have allowed her daughter to behave this way—not without a fight, anyway—nor would she have allowed her daughter to adopt the styles of those who did: the rising hemlines, the wanton strings of pearls. But it wasn't merely a desire to avoid a scene that prevented Beatrice from crossing the threshold. Nor was it guilt. It was fear. Beatrice, as she had been taught by both parents, was afraid to go out there where bad things would happen. As the sexual revolution of the 1920s swirled through the culture, the world became more frightening and the things that could happen seemed infinitely worse.

Wearing Victorian clothes long after styles had changed was Beatrice's way of dealing with the world she had been taught to fear. By wearing the particular costume that she did, she provoked a certain response. People thought she was strange, so they stayed away from her; they didn't intrude. The world kept its distance, and on some level Beatrice felt safe. She would not have felt comfortable otherwise. That's why she didn't suddenly change her ways upon her mother's death. The conditioning remained firmly in place—the inculcated messages about the world. "She was very friendly to us, but that was as far as you could approach her," Beatrice's neighbor Rosamond Hendel said. She would not allow an increasingly unfamiliar world past a certain threshold either.

The Park Avenue flappers eventually got married and pregnant (or vice versa), moved back to Long Island, Westchester or Connecticut and became society matrons. They had practiced only a superficial form of modernity, and for most of them it ended abruptly upon the announcement of their engage-

This magnificent double portrait, which hangs on a wall of the Cliffside Inn parlor is arguably the best known Beatrice Turner painting. It has appeared in countless media stories over the years. It is also the only Beatrice Turner painting that never left the house after Beatrice's death in 1948.

This compelling and sensual study of Beatrice in black was found on a trash heap and rescued by A.J. Sardella and Tony Vasak of Newport.

The elegance of the Victorian detail in this painting is a perfect complement to the innocent wistfulness of a young Beatrice Turner, who painted this self-portrait in her early twenties.

*These two pages consist of
four studies of Beatrice in shades
of blue, spanning a period of some
35 years.*

Her approximate respective ages when she painted these self–portraits were (upper left age 19, lower left age 22, lower right age 54, upper right age 57.

One of the two long-lost paintings that have been "brought back to life." This nearly life-size work was digitally recolorized and electronically recreated by New York artist and graphic designer Kira Eng.

Kira Eng digitally recolorized and recreated this life-size painting, working from a black and white photograph of the original work shot by Newport photographer John Hopf in 1948.

Four non-*portraits by Beatrice Turner. There is growing evidence that she painted a variety of subjects other than herself and her mother.*

Three of the paintings on this page and the preceding were located since 1992, and her recently rediscovered will specifically mentions a number of seascapes and landscapes.

These four paintings have familiar Beatrice Turner subjects but are very much outside of Beatrice's usual treatments. The painting of Mama (1910), left, shows a rare frontal view of Adele. The double portrait, below left, depicts Beatrice and Mama at a tennis match at the Newport Casino. It has something of a late-impressionist aura about it. The painting, below right, shows Mama and Beatrice ready for an unusually formal nighttime occasion.

The painting of Mama to the right has remarkably rich detail and complexity on the exotic urn, as well as in the texture of Adele's gown.

One of the most elegant, formal and colorful of the double portraits, this painting is considerably smaller than the other surviving double portraits, which were often near or at life-size.

*The main Cliffside staircase foyer. Framed and museum-lit Turner artworks
line the walls all the way up to the top of the third floor.*

Cliffside then and now. The black and white photo shows the house c. 1880 with its ballroom wing intact. The color exterior shows Cliffside Inn as it is today, with its newly restored tower. The bottom photo is of Beatrice Turner's own Cliffside bedroom as it appears today, one of the inn's most popular guest rooms.

The tradition of afternoon tea at Cliffside was begun by the Swann family in the 19th century and continued by St. George's School until 1901. The Turners revived the practice in 1907 and maintained it for many years. In 1996 a complete afternoon tea service was revived by the inn for the first time in well over 50 years.

Cliffside Inn today is a seamless blend of Victorian elegance and contemporary luxury.

ment. Beatrice continued to practice her profession. Her modernity was ultimately more substantial—it just never *seemed so* because of the way she dressed.

People who visit the Cliffside Inn and see the self-portraits and double portraits tend to agree with Nat Fleischer who said that Beatrice lived "as strange a life as has ever been lived." Casual observers wonder why Beatrice didn't live a normal life. She would have if she could have. No one ever realized how difficult it must have been for her to function out in the world to the extent she did. But it would be equally mistaken and illusory to conclude from this that she didn't live a happy life.

She *was* happy. One of the few things that can be said about Beatrice Turner with absolute certainty is that she was at times happy to the very depth of her being. If this seems paradoxical or contradictory, read the following passage from "Daily Doings." The setting is the wildflower garden at Cliffside on the morning of September 26, 1927.

> Cut flowers, including a very huge hydrangea more beautifully and faintly flushed with rose pink than any I have hitherto seen. The calendulas also are magnificent (some over three-and-a-half inches across), and out in the dewiness of the morning it was very perfect, with an intoxicating loveliness of imagined spring—that freshness of earth and living which comes only in early autumn in Newport. The bees and crickets fill the air with a continuous hum of content. Yellow butterflies flutter about in hasty aimlessness. The young squirrels race up the branches of the great oak tree, scamper to the very ends of the branches where the acorns grow in a cluster of leaves, turn, clinging, upside-down, their tails suspended in the air, then—the gathering of the acorn achieved—race madly down the aisles of branches and leap floatingly to the lawn, scamper merrily across the grass, stop suddenly, dig madly in the turf with the tiny forepaws, nose the nut in the hole, another frenzied scratching of the tiny paws, a sniff to the earth, and—presto—across the grass in long dancing curves, a leap up the tree trunk, and over again. The movements have the measured gay precision of a dancer.

This passage has such *presence*, you can actually relive a moment in time with Beatrice. You can picture yourself in her garden. You can visualize everything she saw, the objects, textures, colors, and hear everything she heard. You can follow the rapid movements and abrupt pauses of the squirrels as if you were seeing them for yourself. Now ask yourself, how does someone look at things in such a way as to be able to absorb these impressions one morning and then go back inside her house, do this or that, and sometime later that day sit down and recreate the scene so vividly off the top of her head? What is the way of seeing that enables someone to do this?

Ordinarily we look at things in a casual way. We walk into a garden thinking of what happened last night, what we'd like to say to so-and-so, what we're planning to do next year, and where we're going tomorrow. We notice a tree here, a squirrel there and a bed of flowers, and are conscious enough of the general layout of things to navigate to the end of the footpath without bumping into a parked car or the side of a house. Occasionally, we find ourselves thunderstruck by something in our visual field—like a Beatrice Turner painting—and spend a moment or two looking at it more attentively. Then we go right back to imagining what we're going to say tomorrow and what we should've said last night. Beatrice could not have looked at things in a casual way on the morning of September 26, 1927, and written the diary entry found under that date. She had to have another way of seeing.

In *The Wholeness of Nature*, a new book about perception, cognition and modern science, Dr. Henri Bortoft, a British scientist and philosopher of science, has introduced a simple and useful name for this "other way of seeing." He calls it "active seeing," and what he means by this is actively redirecting our attention from what's going on in our minds to what's going on in front of us or around us. Bortoft calls this "plunging into seeing," and the result is something like a meditative experience. One feels not merely aware of one's surroundings, but immersed in them. Shakespeare describes just such an experience in *As You Like It*. The exiled Duke Senior, who has adjusted particularly well to life in Arden forest,

> Finds tongues in trees, books in the running brooks,
> Sermons in stones, and good in everything.

Beatrice Turner, as an artist, trained herself to look at things as compositions. She noticed textures, colors, nuances, details. Habitually immersing herself in her surroundings in this way, through the practice of active seeing, she also found "tongues in trees, books in the running brooks, sermons in stones, and good in everything," and this was the source of her happiness. She was snubbed by the Maud Howe Elliotts of the world. She was not considered one of the "best people." She was not taken seriously as an artist. The Mrs. Marion Eppleys and the Mrs. Admiral William Simses practically refused to shake her hand, and children threw stones at her windows. But she could endure all this and still be happy because she was able to dissociate from high society and, as Henri Bortoft would say, participate in her surroundings.

One of the most compelling passages in her surviving diaries actually suggests Beatrice responding in just this way to a specific indignity. On the evening of July 20, 1927, Beatrice and her mother attended an illustrated lecture at the Art Association of Newport. Washington National Cathedral was then under construction, and Canon Arthur B. Rudd had taken to the lecture circuit to solicit donations for the completion of the building. Canon Rudd, introduced of course by the inevitable Maud Howe Elliott, conveyed through words and pictures a magnificent vision of the finished structure and planned grounds. Beatrice's reaction was characteristically keen:

> There are extensive gardens and among the rare plants a bush or tree that is a slip from a tree at Glastonbury, England, which was originally brought by some saint from the Holy Land and blooms out of season whenever the King of England looks at it or something. Occasionally it blooms at Christmas without the assistance of royal glancing. This was told impressively.

After the presentation, as the crowd filed out of the building, Beatrice overheard people whispering about her.

> Back of us as we left: "Do you see that girl? Well, I'll tell you later!"

Probably a couple of flappers who couldn't wait to murmur about how Beatrice kept her father's body at home so she could paint his portrait in death. These are the very next lines she wrote:

> Beautiful walk home. The tall trees reaching to a deeply black diamond-starred sky, soft furry damp grass beneath the tread, and silence.

Beatrice Turner self–portrait (c. 1947) at age 59.

XII

*E*arly on Sunday evening, September 26, 1948, 54 days after Beatrice Turner died, a strange, burning glow was seen over Newport, Rhode Island. The permanent residents and the members of the summer colony who had not yet left for their winter residences looked up from their Sunday dinners and saw it through their dining room windows, if the windows faced north, or noticed that something had aroused their neighbors. People were looking to the sky, and off in the distance the sky looked as if it were on fire. Hundreds of Newporters walked out their front doors and front gates and followed the glow to the North Dump, and when they got there, they stood transfixed by the sight of a massive blaze. The fire department was called. A crew from Engine Company Number One arrived and decided that as long as the fire wasn't threatening any property, they might as well just let it burn itself out. The Boston Red Sox had been clobbered by the New York Yankees that afternoon. Boston was in a tight pennant race with New York and Cleveland; the Red Sox had started the day on top of the American League, but had fallen into a tie for second place, one game behind the Indians, with five games left in the season. People who might otherwise have been talking about Boston's chances—or Harry Truman's—stood silently by and watched the bonfire burn.

We do not willingly settle for beginnings and middles. We demand endings in our stories. We will allow ourselves to be introduced to a series of events. We will devote a considerable amount of time to following the ramifications of those events—but always in the expectation that the circumstances set in motion at the beginning will eventually resolve themselves into a satisfying conclusion. We go along with a story because we anticipate the pleasant feeling of completion that—we assume—awaits us at the end. From a storytelling point of view, both reader and writer would be well served if the fire of September 26, 1948 were the fire in which thousands of Beatrice Turner's art works were destroyed. Think of it: a beautiful and talented artist dies in obscurity. She leaves a couple *thousand* paintings behind, which no one has any use for. So the paintings are stacked in a heap and burned, but the fire is so big and burns so bright and for so long that it can't be ignored. The whole town comes out to watch, and, in death, she finally receives the undivided attention of everyone who neglected her in life. This ending, if it were the ending, not only satisfies the requirement of completeness, it's also positively classic.

Unfortunately, there's no way of knowing if the fire of September 26th was the Turner estate fire, or if it wasn't. The *Newport Daily News* carried a small item the following day, which said, "A fire that threw up a brilliant reflection that was seen for many miles attracted hundreds of spectators to the area of the North Dump off Admiral Kalbfus road early Sunday evening and led to a call for fire department assistance. The fire," said the *News*, "which apparently had been smouldering for hours, was centered in a great pile of combustible material that had been dumped on the ground a short distance to the east of the incinerator." A reporter from a high school newspaper could have written a more descriptive phrase than "combustible material." It sounds as if the *News* didn't have anyone on the scene Sunday night; the city editor probably debriefed the fire chief over the phone Monday morning. When the fire crew arrived at the dump "in answer to a still alarm at 7:08 PM," the *News* continued, "it found the mound of refuse a mass of flames." The piece ended with the statement that the blaze was allowed to burn itself out. There were no further details.

Oil paints manufactured for the use of artists are made by mixing pig-

This framed and fire-damaged Turner self-portrait was salvaged from another fire, one that occurred in a Newport building many years after the infamous burning of most of Beatrice's lifework at the Newport city dump. It is cherished, nevertheless, by its current owners, as a vivid surviving symbol of the Turner legend.

ments, which in the mixing stage of the process are in powdered form, with a sticky substance to bind the color particles together and make them adhere to the canvas. The standard binder is linseed oil, a vegetable oil. When the oil dries and hardens, it becomes surprisingly flame resistant. Gasoline or kerosene would have to be thrown on the paintings and ignited before the oil would burn. But once the oil did begin to burn, thousands of canvasses, scores of wooden frames, batches of sketches, watercolors and diary volumes, and piles of unsold household furnishings would undoubtedly have produced a rather noticeable and lasting conflagration. However, a massive fire at the city dump wasn't any more uncommon in Newport in 1948 than a mugging in New York today. That's why the item in the *News* was so terse. John Booth, Newport's current fire chief, said, "The incinerator was undersized in those days. Stuff would pile up on the ground and would frequently be ignited by the smouldering hot ash underneath it from a previous fire. The smoke would be seen all over town and draw crowds. Linseed oil is extremely flammable, but you can't connect the newspaper item and Miss Turner's effects without something more to go on."

Since the Truman-era records of the Newport Fire Department also went up in a "mass of flames" in an official housecleaning some years ago, we may have to resign ourselves to the fact that the Beatrice story doesn't have any ending at all. But maybe that's what makes it so interesting. The story never ends and never dies because people like Nathan Fleischer, John Hopf, A. J. Sardella, Tony Vasak, Kay Russell and Win Baker have kept it alive and kept it going. Each of them has found some element of fascination in the woman who preserved her image on canvas so many times, over so long a period of her life. Each has done something to collect and preserve the images and the diaries, and, in so doing, has become part of the continuing story.

By permanently exhibiting all of the extant images, whether original works of art or state-of-the-art reproductions, in one place, the Cliffside Inn, Win Baker has made sure that the legend and legacy of Beatrice Turner will be preserved into the twenty-first century. Cliffside is the only bed-and-breakfast inn in the United States which is also an art museum. Beatrice would be pleased. Baker is also using state-of-the-art technology to further the Beatrice story in ways that even Nathan Fleischer would never have dreamed possible. For years, Baker has toyed with the idea of taking John

Win Baker, owner of Cliffside Inn. The inn's collection displays more than 100 images of Turner art works.

Hopf's black-and-white photographs of some of the missing Beatrice Turner self-portraits, blowing them up and colorizing them roughly the way Ted Turner has colorized classic movies. But using a computer tool to color a suit or a dress or a wall or a tablecloth on an image originally produced in black-and-white is one thing. It is quite another to take a black-and-white photograph of something as textured and dimensional as a portrait in oil, apply color to it and attempt to replicate the rich vision of the fine artist who created the work. Obviously only an advanced process and a person with advanced skills in both the fine arts and computer applications could do this successfully.

By 1997, Baker had found both. Kira Eng is a beautiful young New York artist and graphics designer, an expert in creative image processing who has helped some of the world's most respected architects prepare high-tech presentations. Eng, 30, became intrigued with the idea of restoring a lost painting. She expressly decided not to use artistic license and dab any color she pleased on a black-and-white image. Instead, she studied the extant Turner paintings, closely, intensely, down to the most minute brushstroke, until she developed a feeling for the colors and tones that Beatrice herself had worked with. Kira didn't use her computer until after she used her eyes and mind to recreate Beatrice's palette. Then she took one of Hopf's black-and-white photographs which Win Baker had selected, scanned it into the computer, enhanced the resolution of the image, and began adding to the various parts of the picture the same colors for skin tone, backgrounds, fabrics, etc., that Beatrice Turner had employed on some series of brushstrokes on one or another surviving painting.

The printing process Eng recommended only became widely available nine months before the present writing. DesignWinder is a cutting-edge, ink-jet color printer developed by the LaserMaster Corporation of Eden Prairie, Minnesota. It employs a new wide-format process for printing large-size images intended to be viewed close-up, such as fine arts reproductions. A sheet of paper is mounted on a drum, and, instead of one ink-jet cartridge moving back and forth across the sheet, as in the printers the rest of us own, there are eight cartridges using eight different colors. The drum provides smoother transitions between colors and better precision. The result is the most realistic image that technology can create to date.

The DesignWinder process was used to print a full-size enlargement of the color painting recreated by Kira Eng on her computer screen. The breathtaking image was printed on a large sheet of soft, cotton-fiber paper. The next step in the "cloning" of the lost self-portrait required the multiple talents of a dynamic young man with an improbable name. Gordon Flash, 32, is the grandson of one of the first commercial artists and graphic designers on the island of Jamaica. Flash was born in Jamaica and raised and educated in the U.S. He lives in Connecticut and works in fine custom framing, interior decoration, graphic design and fine arts restoration. Flash mounted the printed Turner image on foamboard, a lightweight, warp-resistant backing material. Then he spread a sheet of fine art canvas over the image and put the covered picture in a hot press. The machine pressed the weave of the canvas onto the picture. Flash then uncovered the artwork, placed a layer of laminating film over it and coated it with a clear compound to give the picture an oil-like sheen. The mixture was his own recipe and is an amalgam of materials widely employed by artists for other purposes, such as Gesso, a substance painters use to prime their canvasses (otherwise the paint would be soaked into the material) and marbling glaze, a smearable gel used to produce marble-like patterns on fabrics. Flash followed Beatrice's actual brushstrokes as he worked the compound over the surface of the image. In this way, he was able to create not only the look, but the texture of an oil painting. The picture was then put back in the hot press to make the coating permanent.

When the work was finally framed by Gordon Flash and displayed in Kira Eng's studio in New York City's Chinatown, the result was mesmerizing. Observers simply could not believe they weren't looking at an original oil painting. The first test was so successful that Win Baker is sponsoring four more Kira Eng recreations of four more missing Beatrice Turner self-portraits. The five paintings together have a special significance. When Nathan Fleischer found them, they were all on the same frame, one canvas stretched over another. The portraits span roughly the last 20 years of Beatrice's life and were all prominently featured in black-and-white in the July 10, 1950 issue of *LIFE* magazine. Almost a half century later, Baker, Eng and Flash will have succeeded in bringing these widely-seen works "back to life." There will certainly be some public exhibitions of the revived self-portraits and probably some attendant publicity.

Kira Eng   *Gordon Flash*

Beatrice started exhibiting a number of her paintings during the last years of her life. In March of 1944 she exhibited a portrait of her old nemesis, Maud Howe Elliott, at the annual oil exhibition of the Plastic Club in Philadelphia. It received more than passing interest. The *Philadelphia Inquirer* said: "Beatrice Turner's delineation of Mrs. Elliott, daughter of Julia Ward Howe, is a creation of outstanding individuality." The *Inquirer's* review of the club's annual watercolor exhibition in January of 1946 includes this comment: "Of notable richness are Beatrice Pastorius Turner's two large portraits painted in an unusual technique, 'Visitor with Cardcase' and 'Lady in Red Feather,' as well as her brilliant still life, 'The Swan in Spring.'" It is entirely possible that the pooh-bahs of the art world may rediscover Beatrice Turner. Certain of her works surely deserve serious attention, such as the flaming self-portrait, which reveals so much about the artist and the times in which she lived.

Beatrice believed that images can communicate with the beholder on a subtle and profound level. She discussed this in her diary. As a portrait artist, she wanted to create images that would speak to and nurture the viewer's own best tendencies. She wanted to portray "faces with nobility of thought and character and earnest endeavor written upon them. Faces set immutably in their cast of character to be revered, admired and loved." This may have influenced her choice of subject matter. Dr. Jeannette Ridlon Piccard, whose portrait Beatrice painted in Newport in 1944, was the first woman to ascend into the stratosphere, piloting a balloon to a record-breaking 57,579 feet in 1934. She received her Ph.D. in 1942, was a consultant to NASA from 1964 to 1970, entered seminary school in 1972 at the age of 77, and, two years later, became of one of the first eleven women to be ordained as priests in the Episcopal Church. The Piccard and Elliott portraits, "Visitor with Cardcase," "Lady in Red Feather" and "The Swan in Spring" have not yet surfaced. At the moment, Beatrice's reputation rests primarily on the self-portraits. Perhaps this is only fitting. She set herself the task of bringing out the best parts of her subjects; she certainly brought out the best parts of herself, otherwise the works would never have survived. Neither Nathan Fleischer, A. J. and Tony, nor anyone else would have had any use for them.

In addition to the diaries, there are two other written records that reveal some essential things about Beatrice Turner. One is her will. Eighteen years before her death, she worked out plans for the disposition of her estate. She wanted her Philadelphia townhouse to be made available to graduates of the Pennsylvania Academy of the Fine Arts for use as studios, free or at a nominal charge. The rest of her assets, including the proceeds of the sale of Cliffside and its contents, would be dispensed as a fund for the maintenance of the property. The Fellowship of the Pennsylvania Academy rejected this bequest, but Beatrice anticipated that this would happen. She further stipulated in her will that if the Fellowship "fails to accept in writing within a year after my death," that the "rest, residue and remainder of my estate" be administered as the Adele Haas Turner and Beatrice Pastorius Turner Memorial Fund for the acquisition of paintings by contemporary American artists for the Philadelphia Museum of Art. Beatrice expected that this bequest would be honored, and it was.

The other document is a poem she cut out of a newspaper in 1934 at the age of 46. It was called "Laggard Love" and apparently spoke to the depths of her yearning. The clipping was found in one of the volumes of her surviving diaries. It reads, in part:

Love, you are late—
Long stood the postern wide
With all my morning-glories twin-
ed; inside
Bird called to bird for mate.
Noon and the sun
And loves of bees and flowers—
With folded hands unclaimed I
marked the hours
That saw my youth undone.

She was a generous and clear-eyed woman. She was a lonely, solitary woman. She was also, however she may have appeared, a woman who had within herself the unique and enviable capacity to remain keenly and funda-mentally *alive* despite frustration, neglect and the mounting inanities of one's time. All of these qualities come through in the self-portraits. That's why these images continue to enchant. That's why people who own them won't part with them, even if they found them on the street.

But whether or not her works are critically received by those appointed to decide what is good and worthy art, one thing is certain. The efforts now being made to further her story will inevitably lead to new developments in the story, because something new always turns up whenever the story receives any kind of exposure at all. This will undoubtedly be the effect of the present writing. People will come forward who had a personal contact with either Be-atrice Turner or Nathan Fleischer, or know someone else who did. In a trunk in an attic somewhere in the United States, someone will find letters written by Beatrice Turner. One of the Philadelphia Cadwaladers, Wetherills or Lip-pincotts will discover a volume or two of the Beatrice Turner diaries that an elderly relative, now deceased, picked up out of curiosity at 2322 Spruce Street just before the executors of the Turner estate disposed of the property. One page, one paragraph of those documents may force us to look at Beatrice in a completely new light. And, of course, some people who read this report or see a feature story on the evening news about the "paintings brought back to life," will turn to the portrait on the living room wall, or in their mother's or grandmother's house, or down in the basement or out in the garage, and they will see a beautiful and elegant woman with a peaches-and-cream complexion and dark, searching eyes, and they will finally know for sure who the "lady in the hat" was.

ACKNOWLEDGMENTS

Owners of original Beatrice Turner art

We thank the following owners of Beatrice Turner paintings and other works of art for making their art available to us for this project: A. J. Sardella, Jr., Anton Vasak, Carol Geary, Susan King, Bettie Sarantos, Jose Salas, Rick Salas, Peppi Mishcon, Marjorie & J. William Winter, David H. Winter, Cheryl Winter, Mary Atwood Sharp, Joan Shand, Kay Russell, C.B. Baukus, Haverford College, The Genealogical Society of Pennsylvania, Core States Bank and Elizabeth & Win Baker.

Photographs

In 1948, noted photographer John T. Hopf preserved on film all of the paintings and other art works of Beatrice Turner saved by Nathan Fleischer from destruction. The pictures used by *LIFE* magazine in its 1950 Beatrice Turner photospread came from this archive as have some 45 of the photographs which appear in this book. All of the photos of Nathan Fleischer and Cliff Lawn were also taken by Mr. Hopf. Because of his avid support for various Beatrice Turner preservation projects, this book has a remarkable display of art and Newport color.

Special acknowledgment is due Will Dunnigan and The Georgian Press, New York, N.Y., who worked with graphic artist Kira Eng in printing her digitally colorized restorations of John Hopf monochrome photographs of original Beatrice Turner paintings which themselves no longer exist.

The present era photographs of Cliffside Inn were made by George Gardner with the exception of the photograph on page 129, which was made by Robyn Ramos. Several of the newly refound Turner paintings were photographed by John Corbett.

Photographs from personal files were made available by A.J. Sardella, Jr., Anton Vasak, Carol Geary, Monique & Leonard Panaggio, Kay Russell, John Hopf, Ezekiel St. John, Paula Smith, Kira Eng and Gordon Flash.

Request for Information

Anyone with any information concerning the life and times of Beatrice Turner, or the whereabouts of her paintings, drawings and writings, please contact the Cliffside Inn, 2 Seaview Avenue, Newport, Rhode Island 02840, (401) 847-1811, (800) 845-1811.

Newport Legends, LLC
Publisher